Classrooms and Courtrooms

FACING SEXUAL
HARASSMENT IN
K–12 SCHOOLS

Classrooms and Courtrooms

FACING SEXUAL
HARASSMENT IN
K–12 SCHOOLS

Nan Stein

FOREWORD BY PAT SCHROEDER

TEACHERS
COLLEGE
PRESS

Teachers College, Columbia University
New York and London

Published by Teachers College Press, 1234 Amsterdam Avenue, New York, NY 10027

An earlier version of Chapter 5 appeared under the title "Is It Sexually Charged, Sexually Hostile, or the Constitution? Sexual Harassment in K-12 Schools" in *West's Education Law Reporter*, *98* (June 1, 1995), 621–631. Reprinted with the permission of West Group.

Portions of Chapters 1 and 2 first appeared in Nan Stein, "Sexual Harassment in School: The Public Performance of Gendered Violence," *Harvard Educational Review*, 65:2 (Summer 1995), pp. 145–162. Copyright © 1995 by the President and Fellows of Harvard College. All rights reserved.

Library of Congress Cataloging-in-Publication Data

Stein, Nan D., 1947–
    Classrooms and courtrooms : facing sexual harassment in K-12
schools / Nan Stein ; foreword by Pat Schroeder.
      p.   cm.
    Includes bibliographical references (p.) and index.
    ISBN 0-8077-3879-4 (cloth : alk. paper).—ISBN 0-8077-3878-6
(pbk. : alk. paper)
    1. Sexual harassment in education—United States.   2. Sexual
harassment—Law and legislation—United States.   3. Actions and
defenses—United States.   4. School violence—United States.
    I. Title.
    LC212.82.S72   1999
    371.7'8—dc21   99-39472

ISBN 0-8077-3878-6 (paper)
ISBN 0-8077-3879-4 (cloth)

Printed on acid-free paper
Manufactured in the United States of America

06   05   04   03   02   01   00   99   8   7   6   5   4   3   2   1

Contents

Foreword

AMERICA EMERGED from the year of special prosecutors, grand jury testimonies, and impeachment proceedings even more confused than ever about what constitutes sexual harassment. I thought it was impossible to throw more confusion into the area, but I was wrong.

Fortunately Nan Stein has written CLASSROOMS AND COURTROOMS: FACING SEXUAL HARASSMENT IN K–12 SCHOOLS to light up the road and help us exit the confusion. This is a book all thinking citizens should read and especially all those associated with schools—school board members, administrators, teachers, parents.

I spent 24 years in the U.S. House of Representatives, and those years also saw the recognition that sexual harassment was a critical issue. When I was sworn into Congress in 1973, no one had ever heard the words *sexual harassment.* Society had opted not to deal with it. Of course, such behavior was going on at all levels of our culture, including the schools, but it was "life." As more women moved into the workplace with greater independence and more education, they insisted something should be done. That doesn't mean that only women can be victims, but they were clearly a majority of the victims and wanted the government to give them leverage to deal with those problems.

As co-chairs of the Congressional Caucus on Women's Issues, Representative (now Senator) Olympia Snowe from Maine and I were the locus and focal point of all legislative issues for women. We helped draft and pushed very hard for adoption of legislation dealing with sexual harassment. Then we were at the center of the storm as the nation began to crack the culture of sexual harassment.

Along with almost every other American, I have been involved in debates about what sexual harassment is and what it is not. We all know this area is a sea of gray, which is still much too large. Different judicial circuits continue to interpret the law in different ways. With her book, Nan Stein gives us a compass to help navigate this sea of gray. We can't turn back. We need clear bright lines instead of confusion.

Obviously, education is the key to getting us out of this quagmire. If young people get a good grounding on how to manage relationships with others at a young age, we're on the right path. There is some talk of surrender "just retreat to same-sex education, study groups, and sports." But that still doesn't preclude legal charges because the courts have ruled that sexual harassment is broad enough to cover same sex discrimination. So we need to get on with grounding people in an understanding of what is permissible behavior toward others.

I am proud of Nan Stein for tackling this difficult subject of sexual harassment. Everyone who reads on will be rewarded by a much deeper understanding of this area of the law.

Pat Schroeder

Acknowledgments

In the beginning and throughout the process of writing this book—which took much longer than I thought it would—there has been a core group of people who never stopped asking about my progress. Typically they would ask me when I didn't want to be asked or when I couldn't escape. These individuals also provided long-term guidance, ideas, reviews, e-mail messages, and many meals, and I want to thank them for their persistence, loyalty, humor, and interest. They include Theresa and Imani Perry, Joe Blatt, David Leshtz, Eleanor Linn, Hilary Goldstine, Sari Knopp Biklen, and Nancy Murray. My parents, Gladys and Joe Stein, also continually wondered about my progress and expressed their interest and support in many ways.

In addition, stretching back many years, several other people made themselves available to me to discuss questions and implications of sexual harassment in and beyond elementary and secondary schools. Among those people whom I would like to thank are Freada Klein, Mary Rowe, Joyce Kaser, Susan Fineran, Pam Chamberlain, Sally Engle Merry, Jackson Katz, Roger Levesque, and Susan Hippensteele.

Moreover, several teachers and guidance counselors around the country served as my reality check as they let me in on their strategies to implement sexual harassment training, policies, and guidelines within their schools. They also were my conduit to students, who are the greatest reality check of all. They include Susan Haines from Anchorage, Alaska; Ellen Makynen from Framingham, Massachusetts; Judy McCarthy from Martha's Vineyard, Massachusetts; and Marg Montgomery from Newton, Massachusetts. I'd have been lost without teachers and the information they provided to me about their strategies to prevent sexual harassment in their schools. Staff from the Human and Civil Rights Division of the National Education Association gave me access to scores of teachers around the nation and I am indebted to them and our collaboration.

Several of my colleagues at the Center for Research on Women at Wellesley College were also helpful in a variety of ways. Susan Bailey, the executive director, kept reassuring me that we would find funding for my research projects and that I should just finish my book. Deborah Tolman was often available to toss around rather avant-garde ideas, whether we agreed or not; our talks, in particular the one we had on "coed-naked T-shirts," were always stimulating, provocative, respectful, and above all, humorous. Nancy Marshall and former Wellesley College student Linda Tropp were instrumental in the analysis of the 2,000 surveys returned to us through our *Seventeen* magazine survey. Pam Baker-Weber calmed me during computer glitches and solved many of them. My two assistants, Christine Barnes and then Barkley Shafer, knew when to keep others away from me when I was furiously writing, and graciously returned all the phone calls that I couldn't during these past several years.

Several lawyers either read various sections of my book when they were previously published in professional journals, or provided me with copies of legal decisions or citations. Those attorneys include Donna Russell, Kathryn Woodruff, Sarah Wunsch, and Gayle Sakowski, as well as staff from the National Women's Law Center in Washington, DC; the law offices of Mary Jo McGrath in Santa Barbara, California; and the California Women's Law Center in Los Angeles. However, if I have made errors, legal or otherwise, they are my own.

Several chapters of my book formed the basis of a report on sexual harassment and sexual violence in schools that I was commissioned to write for the Office of Juvenile Justice and Delinquency Prevention in the U.S. Department of Justice, through the Hamilton Fish National Institute on School and Community Violence, a project housed at George Washington University. I am indebted to Gregg Jackson, Paul Kingery, Janet Humphrey, and Lisa Murphy for providing me with their comments and for obtaining those of several anonymous outside reviewers.

My Wellesley College student assistants, Sonja Jacobsen, Kimberlee Williamson, and Laura Murray, helped with data analysis and technical matters and taught me about the wonders of word processing, interlibrary loan, and the World Wide Web.

Finally, sections of this book are based on research projects, and I am deeply indebted to individual donors, foundations, and federal agencies. My research into bullying, described in Chapter 3, began with a grant from the Patina Foundation in 1992 and was sustained by several individual donors, allowing me to work in several school districts in Massachusetts and ultimately to develop a teaching guide on bullying. I am indebted to seven teachers, one guidance counselor, and three principals in Boston and Brookline, Massachusetts (please refer to *Bullyproof: A Teacher's Guide on Teasing and Bullying for Use with Fourth and Fifth Grade Students*, by Lisa Sjostrom and Nan Stein, published by Wellesley College Center for Research on Women). In 1995, additional funds from the U.S. Department of Education allowed research to continue for kindergarten through Grade 3. For that funding, I would like to thank Educational Equity Concepts in New York City, the prime contractor on our grant. Work in Massachusetts was overseen and analyzed by my valued colleague Nancy Mullin-Rindler at the Center for Research on Women, and our three research assistants Alina Martinez, Debra N. Olshever, and Barbara Wilder-Smith, who interviewed and observed many teachers, principals, parents, and students in the Framingham, Massachusetts, school district.

Moreover, Carole Saltz, executive director of Teachers College Press, has been both patient and prodding, feeding me all along with food, advice, and ideas for many years. Susan Liddicoat, my editor at Teachers College Press, deserves special mention and praise; I wish I could have access to her for every writing project I do.

My dog Maya was my constant companion when I came to the office on Saturdays and national holidays as I slogged away on my book. She never hesitated about going to work on the weekends, and having her there forced me to take breaks and get outside for air and exercise, even in the dead of winter. She died in July 1998, several weeks after I turned in the final draft of my book. Bosco now accompanies me and his youthful antics keep me laughing and alert.

Finally, I have been inspired by all the young people who have made public their experiences of sexual harassment and bullying at school, whether as targets, witnesses, or bystanders. They have shared their hopes, indignation, and laughter. Some of them I know personally, others only by the name of their lawsuits, and thousands more merely as respondents to our *Seventeen* magazine survey. I dedicate my book to those I know and then by proxy to all the others: Christine Franklin, Katy Lyle, Jeffrey and Jonathan Pyle, Sarah Hegland, Erin Rollenhagen, three boys whom I knew as eighth graders from the Newton, Massachusetts, schools, the fourth graders from Boston and the fifth graders from Brookline, Massachusetts, and all the many respondents to our *Seventeen* magazine survey. I wouldn't have a book without them.

Introduction

No LONGER a secret, the subject of sexual harassment was propelled into the national consciousness and discourse in the aftermath of the Clarence Thomas–Anita Hill hearings in October 1991. Five months later, in February 1992, a 9–0 landmark decision in the U.S. Supreme Court in the *Franklin v. Gwinnett County Public Schools* case brought attention to the problem of sexual harassment in K–12 schools. For the first time in the 20-year existence of Title IX, the federal law that guarantees an educational environment free from sex discrimination and, by implication and interpretation, sexual harassment, schools could be held liable for compensatory damages if they fail to provide an educational environment that was free from sex discrimination.[1] In the span of those 5 months, the country received a very public, nationally televised lesson on the subject of sexual harassment in the workplace, followed by a stern warning to the educational community from the U.S. Supreme Court.

However, 6 years later, at the end of the Supreme Court's term (June 22, 1998), they handed down a divided decision (5–4) in the *Gebser v. Lago Vista Independent School District*, in which the school district was not held liable for sex discrimination because the authorities had not had "actual knowledge" of the sexual relationship between a minor female student and a male teacher. This decision can serve to confuse school personnel about their responsibilities regarding adult-to-student sexual harassment in schools as established under the *Franklin* decision in 1992. As Justice John Paul Stevens wrote in his opinion for the dissent, the Court's majority "rank[ed] the protection of the school district's purse above protection of immature high school students" (Opinions in sexual harassment case, 1998, p. 31).

Just before this book went to press, the Supreme Court heard its first peer-to-peer sexual harassment case, *Davis v. Monroe County (GA) School*

1

District (No. 97-843), in January 1999. This pivotal case will hopefully clarify conflicts between the circuit courts and provide needed guidance to school personnel around the country. The timing of the hearing in the Supreme Court made it impossible to discuss the outcome of the case in the body of this book; however, the decision will be discussed in the Epilogue.

The Thomas-Hill hearings raised the nation's collective consciousness about the existence of sexual harassment in the workplace, and the *Franklin* case moved this formerly secret social problem of sexual harassment in K–12 schools out beyond the privacy of the school yard's gates. Yet, just because the subject of sexual harassment tumbles through the halls of Congress and the Supreme Court and into public consciousness doesn't mean that its definitions are any clearer nor its solutions any more obvious. Nor is it immediately apparent how to derive lessons from those public and dramatic events to the less-charged, daily mundane occurrences of sexual harassment in K–12 schools.

In October 1996, the "kiss heard around the world" captured the attention of the media, and thereby the public (O'Toole, 1997; Stein, 1997). The episodes of the kissing 6- and 7-year-olds (Johnathan Prevette in Lexington, in North Carolina, and De'Andre Dearinge in New York City, respectively) served to trivialized and distort the problem of sexual harassment in schools, but also pointed out the dearth of age-appropriate explanations and remedies that currently reside in the repertoire of school administrators. While the nation was caught up in the media storm surrounding these episodes, egregious examples of sexual harassment were in litigation in courtrooms in California and New York state (*Doe v. Antioch (CA) Unified School District*, 1996; and *Bruneau v. South Kortright (NY) Central School District*, 1996), but those two cases received nowhere as much publicity as the kissing among little children.

A reasonable person might ask, Where is the middle ground and how wide is it? Is the only choice between litigious formulations resolved in courtrooms or a silly and absurd conceptualization of sexual harassment that creates tempests in teapots? Others suggest that all we need to do is to "respect" each other and we will be able to rid ourselves of sexual harassment. However tempting such explanations and solutions might be, they belie the fact that different cultures, let alone different people, walk around with divergent measuring sticks for respect, let alone for what constitutes sexual harassment.

However, the people who advocate simplistic solutions also talk about sexual harassment as those behaviors that we all universally recognize as "crossing over the line." Yet, once again, lines are not universal; definitions and understandings are not monolithic. Especially when dealing with adolescents, lines get tested and violated all the time. Leave it to adolescents to try to push the envelope about what is permitted and what is just a bit over the line.

WORKING DEFINITIONS

In this book I will discuss many of the murky aspects of sexual harassment in school—those that do not lie simply beyond and over the lines, but rather, between the lines. At the outset, I am going to suggest that we might be better off if we would recognize that the subject of sexual harassment is ambiguous and complex. Notwithstanding its complexity, we have to start somewhere, so I will propose some working definitions of key terms as they apply largely to the domain of education: sex discrimination, sexual harassment, gender harassment, and gender violence.

Sex Discrimination

Under Title IX of the Education Amendments of 1972, no individual may be discriminated against on the basis of sex in education programs receiving federal financial assistance. Included among the domains are athletic opportunities and funding, guidance and counseling services, admission to courses, and the rights of pregnant and parenting students.

Sexual Harassment

A form of prohibited sex discrimination where the harassing conduct creates a hostile environment, sexual harassment constitutes unwelcome sexual advances, requests for sexual favors, and other verbal or physical conduct of a sexual nature when the conduct is sufficiently severe, persistent, or pervasive to limit a student's ability to participate in or benefit from the education program, or to create a hostile or abusive educational environment. Sexual harassment is unwanted and unwelcome behavior of a sexual nature that interferes with the right to receive an equal educational opportunity. It is a form of sex discrimination that is prohibited by Title IX, a federal civil-rights-in-education law that addresses issues of sex discrimination and, by judicial precedent, sexual harassment.

Both the courts and the Office for Civil Rights of the U.S. Department of Education recognize two forms of unlawful sexual harassment: quid pro quo harassment and hostile-environment harassment. According to the March 13, 1997, Guidance in the *Federal Register*, issued by the Office for Civil Rights, quid pro quo harassment occurs when a school employee explicitly or implicitly conditions a student's participation in an education program or activity or bases an educational decision on the student's submission to unwelcome sexual advances, requests for sexual favors, or other verbal, nonverbal, or physical conduct of a sexual nature. Quid pro quo harassment is equally unlawful whether the student resists and suffers the threatened harm or submits and thus avoids the threatened harm (U.S. Department of Education, 1997a).

On the other hand, hostile-environment harassment, which includes unwelcome sexual advances, requests for sexual favors, and other verbal, nonverbal, or physical conduct of a sexual nature by an employee, by another student, or by a third party, is behavior that is sufficiently severe, persistent, or pervasive to limit a student's ability to participate in or benefit from an education program or activity, or to create a hostile or abusive educational environment (U.S. Department of Education, 1997a). Most typically, in school settings, particularly between students, allegations concern the hostile-environment claim.

According to the OCR Guidance:

> A school will be liable under Title IX if its students sexually harass other students if (1) a hostile environment exists in the school's programs or activities; (2) the school knows or should have known of the harassment; and (3) the school fails to take immediate and appropriate corrective action. . . . A school's failure to respond to the existence of a hostile environment within its own programs or activities permits an atmosphere of sexual discrimination to permeate the educational program and results in discrimination prohibited by Title IX. . . . Title IX does not make a school responsible for the actions of harassing students, but rather for its own discrimination in failing to remedy it once the school has notice. (U.S. Department of Education, 1997a, pp. 12039–12040)

Gender Harassment

This term refers to acts of verbal or physical aggression, intimidation, or hostility based on sex but not involving sexual activity or language; this conduct may be a form of discrimination prohibited by Title IX. Males as well as females may be targets or perpetrators, and the harassment may be directed at members of the same or opposite sex. It is important to note that Title IX's prohibition of sexual harassment does not extend to nonsexual touching or other nonsexual conduct. Incidents of gender-based discrimination can be combined with incidents of sexual harassment to create a hostile environment, even if each by itself would not be sufficient (U.S. Department of Education, 1997a).

Gender Violence

A broader concept, this term includes conduct that may or may not be discriminatory under Title IX. According to the sociologists O'Toole and Schiffman (1997),

> Gender violence is any interpersonal, organizational, or politically oriented violation perpetrated against people due to their gender identity, sexual orientation, or location in the hierarchy. . . . compulsory aggression as a central component of masculinity serves to legitimate male-on-male violence, sexual harassment as a means of controlling the public behavior of women, gay and lesbian bashing. (p. xii)

Among the examples of gender violence in schools are gender-based bullying or hazing rituals that are often imposed upon new members of an athletic team, students who don't conform to conventionality, or the youngest or newest students. Some of the most violent gendered behaviors are those inflicted upon gay or lesbian students or those students who are perceived to be or friendly with those so labeled.

SEXUAL HARASSMENT ACCORDING TO THE MEDIA

The popular media, on the other hand, have created a very different definition of sexual harassment. Upon the discovery that the subject resonates with the public, it has become the subject of television talk shows, news magazine shows, made-for-television productions, and much column space in the popular and educational press. In large part both the educational and popular press's attention to the problem of sexual harassment in schools has been generated by the lawsuits and the surveys on sexual harassment in schools.

However, if it is left to the popular media to define sexual harassment, we come away with the notion that it besets only girls, and is perpetrated solely by boys. Moreover, girls are portrayed as victims, as frail and whiney, or on the other hand, as seductive and manipulative; whereas boys are cast as sufferers of hormones run amok or as playful creatures engaging in harmless fun that is misunderstood by adults and by girls.

Moreover, this world of sexual harassment as created by the popular media is divided into two camps—that of the target, and that of the perpetrator; there is no in-between or movement back and forth, nor do any other groups exist. Any way we look at this construct, we are provided with a one-dimensional, rigid framework, filled with misconceptions and distortions that leave out the role or vantage point of the bystanders, witnesses, and observers of sexual harassment, and almost never report on boys' experiences of sexual harassment.

Most of the major talk and television news shows have had programs that focus on sexual harassment in schools. From *Oprah* (4/19/93; 10/21/96) and *Donahue* (4/15/92) to the minor leagues of talk shows, many of which have come and gone, such as *A Closer Look with Faith Daniels* (8/92), *Night Talk with Jane Whitney* (4/17/92; 2/3/93), *Sally Jesse Raphael* (9/15/94), and *Leeza* (9/12/96), these shows, almost without exception, have portrayed sexual harassment as an event or phenomenon that pits girls against boys— girls as targets, boys as perpetrators. Solutions other than lawsuits are rarely discussed; students who understand the problem are missing from the depictions of students' cultures and subcultures; and emotional outbursts from the audience and panelists are preferred and solicited over reasoned discourse.

In addition, most of the network morning news shows, including ABC's *Good Morning, America*, and NBC's *Today Show*, and several of the news magazine shows, including CBS's *Eye to Eye With Connie Chung* (6/17/93), Fox's *Front Page* (9/25/93), NBC's *Dateline NBC* (9/15/96), and ABC's *Nightline with Ted Koppel* (6/18/93; 10/4/96) have had segments on sexual harassment in schools. Though less emotional and irrational, these shows nonetheless portray the world as divided in two camps—harassers and targets—and often describe this bifurcated state as inevitable. Furthermore, there have been several after-school and made-for-television specials aimed at a youth audience on the subject of teenage sexual harassment,[2] and these shows have usually focused on one lawsuit or another, typically with a teenage girl going against her peers and naming a popular boy (or male teacher) as the harasser.

At the same time, the subject has been covered in a wide variety of magazines and journals. Discussion of this issue has not been left to *Ms.* magazine, academic feminist journals, or law review articles—the subject has moved from the margins to become a mainstream concern. Articles have appeared in a wide variety of newspapers and magazines that are aimed at the general public as well as directed at teenagers, women, and parents.[3] But, airtime and column space alone do not necessarily guarantee greater understanding of the problem.

A variety of professional education journals and periodicals have carried articles on sexual harassment in K-12 education that provide a more complex, nuanced, and accurate picture of the problem. Unfortunately, these journals are typically read solely by educators and graduate students, not by the general public, so the oversimplifications and myths remain largely untouched and embedded.[4]

MY PERSPECTIVE AND VANTAGE POINTS

I come to the subject of sexual harassment in schools from several perspectives and vantage points. I first learned of the experiences of sexual harassment from listening to high school students (1979), then surveying them, first in Massachusetts (1980–81), and then from all over the country (in 1992 through *Seventeen* magazine; Stein, Marshall, & Tropp, 1993); and developing curriculum on the subject (*Who's Hurt and Who's Liable: Sexual Harassment in Massachusetts Schools* [Stein, ed.], first published in 1979 and revised in 1981, 1982, 1983, and 1986; *Flirting or Hurting? A Teacher's Guide on Student-to-Student Sexual Harassment in Schools* in 1994 [Stein & Sjostrom, 1994]; *Bullyproof: A Teacher's Guide on Teasing and Bullying for Use with Fourth and Fifth Grade Students* [Sjostrom & Stein, 1996]; and *Gender Violence/Gender Justice: An Interdisciplinary Teaching Guide for Teachers of English, Literature, Social Studies, Psychology, Health, Peer Counseling, and Family and Consumer Sciences* (*Grades 7–12*) [Stein & Cappello, 1999]). Wherever students have led me, both physically and conceptually, I have tried to go.

As an educator and practitioner, a former middle school social studies teacher, and a drug and alcohol counselor, I have surrounded myself for many years with teachers and administrators, immersing myself in their classrooms, hallways, lunchrooms, departmental meetings, and those required in-service training sessions held on early-release days. Whenever possible, I continue to work in classrooms with students and their teachers. Over these many years, and often in conjunction with teachers, I have developed curriculum materials and teaching guides. I am at once a practitioner, writer, researcher, activist, and reluctant theorist.

However, a glaring omission in my work is the articulation of race. I cannot invent information about the relevance of sexual harassment in the lives of students of African American, Asian, Native American, or Latin American descent, nor will I extend what I have learned from nearly 2 decades of research into sexual harassment to apply to teens of color if they have not been part of the research. For example, in our *Seventeen* magazine survey, only 10% of the respondents were racial minority females (see Chapter 1); in the American Association of University Women (AAUW) study (1993), minority students made up 35% of the sample. Moreover, of the dozens of complaints or lawsuits that are not anonymous, very few have been filed by girls of color (LaShonda Davis, an African American female, in Georgia; and Tiana Urgarte, a Chicana, in Antioch, California, are the two major exceptions—see Chapter 2). However, it may as well be the case that access to resources, which includes both lawyers to hire and public agencies to act on one's behalf, may account for some of the imbalance between lawsuits filed by European Americans and those filed by racial minority families. Nonetheless, there is no shortage of lawsuits and complaints that have been filed by racial minority adult women about workplace discrimination and harassment. So, the question to ponder becomes, Why not school-aged females?

Although I have no definitive research to which to refer, I do have some hunches about the absence of young African American, Native American,

Latina, and Asian students in this debate about sexual harassment in schools. My hypotheses include several: that racial minority students do not trust the system of justice as practiced by school personnel, so they do not report incidents; that young racial minority women do not want to get their male counterparts in trouble with school personnel; and that some racial minority girls are able to deal with the problems of sexual harassment on their own, and in many cases do not view the interactions as sexual harassment, but rather as mutual, sexual or otherwise, banter. In the 1991 self-esteem study commissioned by the AAUW, young African American women reported and retained higher self-esteem throughout adolescence than did White and Latina females (AAUW, 1991; Ward, 1996), and a greater "talk-back" repertoire (Smith, 1994).

To say that more research is needed on how, if, and the many ways that young people of color understand and experience sexual harassment is a gross understatement.

OVERVIEW OF BOOK

This book is about sexual harassment in K–12 schools. I will draw from legal, anecdotal, and survey research as well as from incidents described in the popular and educational press. At times we will reside in the realm of generalizations, only to switch to the particulars of one person's lawsuit or circumstances or travel to one school's or one teacher's efforts to teach about sexual harassment. What might seem inconsistent or contradictory may well be, but the lack of logic so far hasn't stopped contradictions from coexisting in schools. This book is a journey through schools and not an ethnography or microanalysis of one school.

The book is organized as follows: In Chapters 1 and 2, material from surveys and salient lawsuits as well as anecdotal information from students immerses the reader in the everyday culture of sexual harassment in schools, and points out the contradictions and confusions that coexist, whether imposed by school administrators or the courts. Chapter 3 focuses on gender-based bullying and sexual harassment among children in elementary schools. I offer background information on a variety of both large- and small-scale research studies on bullying that have been conducted around the world, and attempt to answer the question, Is bullying sexual harassment? Chapter 4 continues the discussion about confusion over words, focusing on the misapplication and the overapplication of the term *sexual harassment* for sex discrimination. In Chapter 5 I explore the gendered application of the First Amendment rights of students, such that girls are afforded fewer and more restrictive expressive rights, often in the name of prevailing notions of sex-role-typical behaviors and expectations. In Chapter 6 I trace justice and miscarriages of justice in the schoolhouse when administrators attempt to adjudicate sexual harassment disputes among students. In Chapter 7 I present disturbing trends in schools as the sites of sexual violence, and suggest directions for more research to determine to what extent sexual harassment in schools is occurring between students who are or had been dating, or where one person desires to be in a dating relationship but the second party is not interested. Some of the peer sexual harassment lawsuits would lead one to believe that longtime acquaintanceships or friendships grew into sexual harassment as the boy wanted to escalate that relationship with the girl into a dating relationship, but the girl did not want to become more intimate or involved with the boy. Moreover, in this final chapter I will present data from several sources, including national crime-victim surveys that locate schools as the sites of sexual violence. The book ends with a set of recommendations to reduce sexual harassment and sexual violence in schools.

Sexual Harassment in Schools: Surveys Reveal the Public Performance of Gendered Violence

"Ask Beth," the nationally syndicated teenage-advice column, often prints letters from youngsters in which they describe their experiences of sexual harassment in schools. On February 3, 1994, the column in the *Boston Globe* contained this letter:

> Dear Beth: I am 11 years old and there's a boy in my class who just won't leave me alone. He chases after me and my best friend during recess. He hits and kicks me on the behind, stomach and legs. Once he slapped me so hard it brought tears to my eyes. I try to tell my teacher, but she just laughs and tells him, "If you like her so much, ask her for her phone number." Is this sexual harassment? If it is, what should I do?
>
> HATES BEING HARASSED (Winship, 1994, p. 50)

When I read this letter aloud to middle school and high school students from around the country, from Maryland to Alaska, and ask them, "If these people were older, what might we call these behaviors?" I receive answers such as "dating violence," "assault," "domestic violence," and "stalking." These students clearly know what is going on, and do not pull any punches when naming or describing it. Yet, the teacher mentioned by the letter writer either infantilized the assaultive behaviors, maybe choosing to perceive them as flattery or as efforts from youthful, albeit primitive, suitors, or chose to dismiss the problem of sexual harassment—"If I don't see it, it's not happening."

In this chapter on sexual harassment in schools I will document the phenomenon as recorded through a multitude of surveys, echoed by the voices of adolescents and the reactions from school personnel. A collective portrait emerges of the almost mundane, commonplace nature of sexual harassment in schools. From students' written narratives as well as results from many surveys, including two national ones conducted in 1993 (the *Seventeen* magazine study and the AAUW survey), and a third in 1996 (*USA Weekend*); and several surveys that are state specific (Massachusetts, 1980–1981; Iowa, 1994; Connecticut, 1995; New Jersey, 1994–1996; North Dakota, 1997; and Texas, 1997), a widespread, endemic phenomenon of sexual harassment emerges. These surveys, on the one hand, point out that sexual harassment is a very public event; yet, on the other hand, the results demonstrate that school personnel often treat sexual harassment among students as if it is a hidden, secret phenomenon.

Moreover, the stories that surface from narratives, and surveys documenting the experiences of or observations from both boys and girls in K–12 schools illustrate that sexual harassment has become normalized as its public performance is tolerated, even expected, and allowed to flourish. A school culture has been created that gives, in effect, permission to proceed, potentially turning schools into practice fields and training grounds for dating/domestic violence and other forms of interpersonal gender violence (Stein, 1995a), as I explore later in the book.

Since 1993, there have been a handful of surveys on sexual harassment in schools: three national surveys, six that have been state specific, and the remainder those solely based at one school. A few studies have surveyed gay, lesbian, and bisexual students; and only one small pilot survey considered the experiences of students with disabilities. For each survey I summarize its findings and indicate the limitations, as well as generalizability. My review will demonstrate that the evidence points toward a well-substantiated conclusion that sexual harassment is a pernicious, persistent, and public problem.

NATIONAL SURVEYS

Results from three national surveys of sexual harassment in schools illustrate the nature of sexual harassment in schools and demonstrate a widespread, endemic phenomenon.

Seventeen Magazine Survey (1993)

The September 1992 issue of *Seventeen* magazine contained an article (LeBlanc, 1992) on the sexual harassment of a girl in high school, which appeared along with a survey that consisted of 11 multiple-choice and two open-ended questions. At the time, *Seventeen* was the most widely read magazine for teenage girls in the country, with 1.9 million subscribers, and a "pass along" circulation of 8–10 million girls ("Study Calls Schools Lax on Sexual Harassment," 1993). This first survey instrument was written by the Wellesley College Center for Research on Women and cosponsored by the NOW Legal Defense and Education Fund. The results were compiled from a nonprobability, random sample of 2,002 girls aged 9–19, selected from a total of 4,300 surveys received by the deadline of September 30, 1992, and were released in March 1993 (Stein, Marshall, & Tropp, 1993). No boys responded to the survey, which comports to the readership data of the magazine.

The girls' responses revealed the tenacity and pervasiveness of sexual harassment in schools. Surveys by the thousands, screaming with messages scribbled on envelopes, "Open," "Urgent," "Please Read," and handwritten on lined notebook paper or on perfumed stationery—all begged for attention, for answers, and above all, for some type of acknowledgment and justice (Stein, 1995a).

Three major themes emerged from these testimonials, all of which were voluntary elaborations on the open-ended questions "What do you think schools should do to prevent sexual harassment?" and "If you've been sexually harassed at school, how did it make you feel?" The themes were

1. The public nature of sexual harassment, revealing that there were bystanders and observers to these events, some of whom were adult employees of the school
2. That the targets of the harassment were not passive in the face of this harassment, thereby belying the stereotypic notion that girls are passive victims
3. That when the girls told school officials about the sexual harassment incidents, their stories were often dismissed or trivialized

The data from the survey demonstrated that the most common forms of sexual harassment were receiving sexual comments, gestures, or looks (reported by 89% of the girls); and being touched, pinched, or grabbed (reported by 83% of the girls). Sexual harassment was not a one-time-only event: 39% of the girls reported being harassed on a daily basis during the past year. In two thirds of the incidents of sexual harassment reported in the *Seventeen* study, the girls indicated that other people were present.

The good news, however, was that the girls and young women were not passive in the face of all the harassment. Almost two thirds told their harassers to stop, more than one third resisted with physical force, and others told their friends, parents, or teachers.

The most frequently cited location of witnessed incidents was the classroom: 94% of the girls who indicated that others were present when harassment occurred reported that it occurred in the classroom; 76% of those who reported that other people were present during the harassment cited the hallway; and 69% cited the parking lot or the playing fields (respondents often cited more than one location).

The limitations of this study are obvious: It is not scientific or random; respondents were limited to motivated readers of the magazine who had all experienced sexual harassment; the ethnic breakdown corresponded only to the ethnic and racial breakdown of the magazine's readership and was not reflective of the nation or of those who experience sexual harassment; and the respondents were entirely female. There is no way to generalize from these findings.

Listening to the Respondents. Among the eloquent statements received as part of the *Seventeen* survey were the following excerpts (ethnic and racial descriptors that accompany the quotes are drawn from the words used by the girls to describe their racial/ethnic background):

> Of the times I was sexually harassed at school, one of them made me feel really bad. I was in class and the teacher was looking right at me when this guy grabbed my butt. The teacher saw it happen. I slapped the guy and told him not to do that. My teacher didn't say anything and looked away and went on with the lesson like nothing out of the ordinary had happened. It really confused me because I knew guys weren't supposed to do that, but the teacher didn't do anything. I felt like the teacher (who was a man) betrayed me and thought I was making a big deal out of nothing. But most of all, I felt really bad about myself because it made me feel slutty and cheap. It made me feel mad too because we shouldn't have to put up with that stuff, but no one will do anything to stop it. Now sexual harassment doesn't bother me as much because it happens so much it almost seems normal. I know that sounds awful, but the longer it goes on without anyone doing anything, the more I think of it as just one of those things that I have to put up with. (14-years-old, White, Spokane, Washington) (Stein, 1995a, p. 146)

> In my case there were 2 or 3 boys touching me, and trust me they were big boys. And I'd tell them to stop but they wouldn't! This went on for about 6 months until finally I was in (one) of my classes in the back of the room minding my own business when all of them came back and backed me into a corner and started touching me all over. So I went running out of the room and the

teacher yelled at me and I had to stay in my seat for the rest of the class. But after the class I told the principal, and him and the boys had a little talk. And after the talk was up, the boys came out laughing cause they got no punishment. (12-years-old, Mexican-American, Saginaw, Michigan) (Stein, Marshall, & Tropp, 1993, p. 10A)

Finally, I got the courage to do something about it. I told my principal what was happening. He was very skeptical about the whole thing, and he didn't do much about it. I wish I knew I was being harassed and had done something more about it . . . but I still felt like it was my fault, and I still do a little bit. (14-years-old, White, a small town in Pennsylvania) (p. 9A)

It made me feel cheap, like I was doing something I wasn't aware of to draw this kind of attention to myself. I could never stand up to him because if I told him to stop he'd threaten me, so I began to act like it didn't bother me . . . he'd hit me (hard enough to bruise me twice) and then pin my arms behind my back till it hurt and push against a wall and tell me all the awful things he would do to me if I ever hit him again, so I quit standing up to him again. (14-years-old, White, small town in Michigan) (Stein, 1992a, p. 23)

At first I didn't really think of it because it was considered a "guy thing," but as the year went on, I started to regret going to school, especially my locker, because I knew if I went I was going to be cornered and be touched, or had some comment blurted out at me. I just felt really out of place and defenseless and there was nothing I could do. (14-years-old, Black, Maryland) (Stein, 1995a, p. 147)

It was like fighting an invisible, invincible enemy alone. I didn't have a clue as to what to do to stop it, so I experimented different approaches. Ignoring it only made it worse. It made it easier for them to do it, so they did it more. Laughing at the perpetrators during the assaults didn't dent the problem at all, and soon my friends became tired of doing this. They thought it was a game. Finally I wrote them threatening letters. This got me in trouble but perhaps it did work. I told the school administrators what had been happening to me. They didn't seem to think it a big deal, but they did talk to the three biggest perpetrators. The boys ignored the administrators and it continued. And they were even worse. (14–15-years-old, White, Worcester, Massachusetts) (Stein, Marshall, & Tropp, 1993, p. 7A)

Seeing Is Not Believing. These chilling stories reveal that sexual harassment in schools has become ordinary, expected, and public. Rarely confined to private, "secret" interactions, sexual harassment takes place most commonly in full and plain view of others. Girls recognize that incidents of sexual harassment are often witnessed by adults, and expect adults to see and feel these violations as they do. Yet, many girls cannot get confirmation of their experiences from school personnel because most of those adults do not name it as sexual harassment and do nothing to stop it (Stein, 1992a). Yet, these stories also demonstrate girls' repeated efforts to get the adults to see and believe what is happening right before their eyes, and to do something about it. Ominously, these young women begin to sound like battered women who are not believed or helped by the authorities and who feel very alone and abandoned. Statements gleaned from the open-ended questions from the *Seventeen* magazine survey on sexual harassment point to this troubling connection, although there are no longitudinal studies that establish such a connection. Listen again to the narratives from the girls responding to the *Seventeen* magazine survey:

> I feel very terrible. I felt it was my fault, but it wasn't. I didn't tell teachers or the principal what happened. I think my problem is being scared. I'm scared they're going to do something worse if I tell. (12-years-old, Mexican-American, Texas) (Stein, 1992a, p. 23)

> I also felt embarrassed and mad, but as if it were my fault by being nice or just letting it continue by doing nothing. (14-years-old, Mexican-American, Texas) (p. 23)

> I grow angry, sad, and I had wanted to get back at him . . . I was very speechless and quiet for sometime, I felt like crying but, I kept it inside and didn't say anything to anyone. (12-years-old, Chinese-American, New York City) (p. 23)

> Being harassed makes me angry and I feel degraded. I'm always on my guard trying to prevent what may happen next. (13-years-old, African-American, Texas) (p. 22)

> Sometimes, I would look at the teacher and think "help," but I was afraid to say anything because maybe it wasn't as bad as I thought it was. (15-years-old, White, South Carolina) (Stein, 1995a, p. 147)

> The guys would want you to let them touch you all over. But I was one of the girls that would not do that. Then one day they thought they would do it anyway. So I defended myself like you should. I kind of hurt him. The teacher caught me hitting him. And I got in trouble for hitting him. The teacher took him out of the room for his story and he lied and said he did nothing. My teacher wouldn't believe my story. I was the one getting in trouble. The school and the principal wouldn't listen to me. (13-years-old, Mexican, Wichita, Kansas) (Stein, Marshall, & Tropp, 1993, p. 7A)

These stories suggest injustices of a magnitude not yet widely considered—that schools may be training grounds for the insidious cycle of domestic violence: Girls are trained to accept this battering and assault and are taught that they are on their own, that the adults and others around them will not believe or help them. Similarly, boys receive permission, even training, to become batterers. Girls (and sometimes boys) who are the targets of sexual harassment find that when they report sexual harassment or assault, the events will be trivialized, but they are demeaned or interrogated or both. Harassers, on the other hand, get the message that, since adults around them fail to intervene, they have tacit permission to continue with their assaults. Indeed, if school authorities do not intervene and instead sanction the students who sexually harass, the schools may be encouraging a continued pattern of violence in relationships. The consequences of this acceptance of sexual harassment goes beyond those directly involved; a message is sent to those who observe, or hear about it later, that to engage in sexual harassment is permissible. Other bystanders may receive the message that they may be the next to be harassed, and no one will do anything to prevent it (Stein, 1992a). Although there has been no research that links child/adolescent sexual harassment to battering later in life, these normalized and public performances of harassment, assault, and battery in schools may have consequences for the privatized relationships that these youngsters will construct later in their lives.

We will return to this disturbing theme and connection throughout the book, especially as we explore the rising nature of violence in teenage relationships (whether dating in fact or in fiction).

Hostile Hallways: The AAUW Survey (1993)

The second survey, *Hostile Hallways*, released in June 1993, was conducted by Louis Harris and Associates, Inc., in partnership with Scholastic, Inc., with funding from the American Association of University Women Foundation. This rigorous survey firmly established that there was an universal culture of sexual harassment with no significant racial differences flourishing in America's secondary schools.

Hostile Hallways randomly sampled 1,632 boys and girls (828 boys and 779 girls), with an oversampling of African American and Hispanic students (15% African American students: 120 African American females and 138 African American males; and 9% Hispanic students: 70 Hispanic females and 78 Hispanic males), in grades 8–11 in 79 public schools. A random sample of schools was selected from the database of public schools at the National Center for Education Statistics with a proportionally drawn sample by grade and regional location. The study can be generalized to all U.S. public schools in grades 8–11. The survey has a 95% confidence level, with a margin of error at plus or minus 4 percentage points.

The survey consists of 40 questions and addresses sexual harassment with regard to the following areas: frequency of experience and perpetration; type (physical and nonphysical); grade level of first experience; frequency of adult to student; frequency of peer to peer; location; impact on students' education (cutting classes or school absence, not wanting to talk as much in class, finding it hard to pay attention or study, thinking about changing schools, etc.); emotional state (such as feeling embarrassed, self-conscious, afraid, confused, more/less popular, etc.) and behavior (avoiding the harasser, staying away from particular places in school, changing your seat, changing friends, route, etc.).

The overall picture of sexual harassment is revealed in Table 1.1. Interestingly, the respondents revealed a similar portrait to that of the *Seventeen* survey of sexual harassment, one that included public incidents occurring throughout the school. Of the 81% of the students who reported some experience of sexual harassment in school, 66% said they had been harassed at least once in the hall; 55% reported the classroom as the site of the harassment; 43% reported occurrences outside of school but on school grounds (other than the parking lot); 39% reported harassment in the gym, playing field, or pool area; 34% indicated the cafeteria as the location; and 23% named the parking lot as the site of the harassment. Students indicated that locker rooms (19%) and rest rooms (10%), presumably gender-segregated sites, were also locations for sexual harassment. Overall, 83% of the girls and 60% of the boys reported experiencing unwanted sexual attention in school.

Table 1.1. Types of Sexual Harassment Experienced in School

	Boys	Girls
Sexual comments, jokes, gestures, or looks	56%	76%
Touched, grabbed, or pinched in a sexual way	42%	65%
Intentionally brushed up against in a sexual way	36%	57%
Flashed or mooned	41%	49%
Had sexual rumors spread about them	34%	42%
Had clothing pulled at in a sexual way	28%	38%
Shown, given, or left sexual pictures, photographs, illustrations, messages, or notes	34%	31%
Had their way blocked in a sexual way	17%	38%
Had sexual messages/graffiti written about them on bathroom walls, in locker rooms, etc.	18%	20%
Forced to kiss someone	14%	23%
Called gay or lesbian	23%	10%
Had clothing pulled off or down	17%	16%
Forced to do something sexual other than kissing	9%	13%
Spied on while dressing or showering	8%	7%

Source: Reprinted with permission from AAUW, *Hostile Hallways*, 1993, p. 9.

One notable limitation of this study is that it asked students to recall all of their sexual harassment experiences during their entire school history and then to focus on the most severe event. The focus on the worst incident may have distorted the nature and severity of the harassment most commonly experienced. Moreover, the definition provided to the students taking the survey was "unwanted and unwelcomed sexual behavior which interferes with your life." This definition has been criticized as too broad ("with your life"), as opposed to one that restricts the students' reflecting upon those behaviors that were only school based. In addition, no information was provided on disabled or gay/lesbian youth, and no socioeconomic-status (SES) data were provided.

According to the analysis of the AAUW poll by Lee, Croninger, Linn, and Chen (1996), the frequency of harassment depends on gender; frequency did not depend on race, ethnicity, or class, or on whether the school environment is one that contains harassment. Other factors with high (plus or minus .001) statistical significance that contributed to one's likelihood of being harassed included having friends who are harassed, having engaged in harassment, and the perception of harassment at one's school (Lee et al., 1996).

Moreover, the severity of harassment is related to gender and race, whether the harassment came from an adult, and whether the school environment tolerated harassment (Lee et al., 1996). Girls are harassed more severely than boys, Blacks more severely than other racial groups, and students in the higher grades more severely than those in the lower (eighth) grades (Lee et al., 1996). Harassment by adults made up a big difference in the severity of sexual harassment experienced by the students. Gender again played a major role: "While harassment by a principal or fellow student did not vary by gender, female students were significantly more likely than their male counterparts to report harassment by a teacher (20% v. 8%) or by a staff member (48% vs. 37%)" (Lee et al., 1996, pp. 400–401).

Furthermore, more than half (53%) of the students reported both harassing and being harassed by their peers. Two thirds (66%) of all boys and more than half (52%) of all girls admitted that they had sexually harassed someone in a school setting. The survey listed the following options: "It's just part of school life" (37% of perpetrators; gender breakdown was 41% boys and 31% girls); "I thought the person liked it" (25% of all perpetrators; gender breakdown of 27% boys and 23% girls); "I wanted a date with the person" (22% of all perpetrators; gender breakdown of 24% boys, 20% girls); "My friends encouraged me/pushed me into doing it" (19% of all perpetrators with no gender gap); "I wanted something from that person" (18% of all perpetrators; gender breakdown of 20% boys, 16% girls); and "I wanted the person to think

I had some sort of power over them" (6% of the perpetrators, gender break-down of 6% of boys and 7% of girls). Unfortunately, no options were provided on the survey that would allow us to understand if the sexual harassment was done in self-defense, thereby leaving open the question about retaliatory/ harassing back as a response to the initial harassment or violence. Another study is needed to figure out which/who came first.

Only 15% of the girls and 31% of the boys in the AAUW sample reported that their lives were untouched by sexual harassment (never been harassed and never harassed others); 31% of girls and 7% of boys indicated that they had been harassed but never had harassed others; and 1.4% of girls and 9.3% of boys said they had never been harassed though they had harassed others.

USA Weekend Magazine Survey (1996)

The third national survey of 222,653 students (44% male and 56% female), released by *USA Weekend* on September 8, 1996, again found that sexual harassment is a very common experience among students (Pera, 1996). This nonprobability survey reflected only the opinions of those students in Grades 6–12 who either were administered the survey by their classroom teachers as part of Channel One programming or chose to respond to the version that was published in 465 newspapers across the country during the last 2 week-ends of March 1996. About two thirds of the responses came from students replying directly to the magazine's survey, whereas one third came from the teacher's guide to Channel One (J. Sexton, personal communication, 1996).

Among the girls, 81% indicated that they had experienced some form of sexual harassment, and 19% reported that they had not experienced sexual harassment at school. For the boys, 76% reported some sort of experience of sexual harassment at school, whereas 24% reported no such experiences at school.

Summary of National Surveys

Despite the nonscientific nature of the *Seventeen* magazine and *USA Week-end* magazine surveys, their findings are strikingly similar to the findings of the scientific AAUW poll.

At least four important findings emerged from the national surveys: (1) Sexual harassment is pervasive in secondary schools (experienced by 83% of the girls and 60% of the boys in the AAUW poll study, 89% of the girls in the *Seventeen* survey, and 81% in the *USA Weekend* survey); (2) students consider sexual harassment a serious problem (75% from the AAUW poll survey, 70% in the *Seventeen* survey); (3) the behavior occurs in public places (two thirds of the situations reported in both the *Seventeen* and AAUW poll studies); and (4) students have difficulty getting help, even though a majority in both the *Seventeen* and AAUW poll surveys reported trying to talk to someone about the harassing behavior.

STATE-SPECIFIC SURVEYS AND SCHOOL-BASED STUDIES

There have been several state-based surveys (Connecticut, Massachusetts, Iowa, North Dakota, New Jersey, and Texas), with varying methodologies, sample sizes, and reliability, some of which have been published whereas others are more obscure and less widely known. Many other people have conducted surveys that have focused solely on one school at a time. Some of those surveys were begun by college or doctoral students. All are included in the Appendix because they indicate that the problem of sexual harassment is recognized as one worthy of study by researchers, school officials, and presumably the parents who gave permission for their children to participate in the study. However, a few important surveys are discussed in this chapter.

Connecticut (1995)

The most scientific of the state-based surveys was conducted by the state of Connecticut during the 1993–94 school year and released in January 1995, titled *In Our Own Backyard: Sexual Harassment in Connecticut's Public High Schools* (Permanent Commission on the Status of Women, 1995).

Seven school districts that the Connecticut Department of Education determined to be representative of socioeconomic status and age were selected. Public high school students totaling 547 in Grades 10 through 12 completed surveys: 308 females and 235 males (four students did not indicate their gender). Demographic characteristics described the sample as 78% Caucasian, 8% African American, 6% Latino, and 4% Asian. No age range or SES information was provided.

When answering the survey questions, students were asked to pick the most upsetting sexually harassing behavior that had happened to them since starting high school. Seventy-eight percent of students surveyed experienced at least one incident of sexual harassment (92% female and 57% male). The study found that girls were nearly twice as likely to experience the problem as boys: 92% of the female students and 57% of the male students reported that they had been the targets of unwelcome sexual conduct since they started high school (Carlson, 1995; Potopowitz, 1995). Other key findings include the following: in 57% of the cases the perpetrator was a single person, though 24% of the students indicated that a group caused the most upsetting behavior. Interestingly, the perpetrator was identified as a friend (33%) or acquaintance (35%) rather than a stranger (9%). A small number (3.5%) of the most upsetting behaviors were perpetrated by school personnel.

The 30 questions on the survey focused on the following areas: frequency, type (physical and nonphysical), frequency of adult to student, frequency of student to student, relationship with harasser (friend, stranger, boyfriend/girlfriend, teacher, coach), location, impact on student's education (cutting classes or school absence), emotional state, behavior (avoiding the harasser) and reporting the harassment.

A strength of this study is that this is a representative sample of the Connecticut school population. Study limitations include lack of analysis by SES, race, and age demographics; and asking students to focus on the most upsetting behaviors/events that occurred only since attending high school. No information was provided on disabled or gay/lesbian youth.

New Jersey (1996)

The New Jersey study, initially undertaken by a group of undergraduates in a research-methods class at Rutgers University in October 1993, examined 696 students (365 girls and 331 boys) from nine schools, distributed in health/family classes, which are required courses (Trigg & Wittenstrom, 1996). The convenience sample was overrepresentative of New Jersey's racial population, but also overrepresented middle- and upper-class communities. The breakdown of the students by grade were as follows: 8% eighth graders; 29% ninth graders; 22% tenth graders; 38% eleventh graders; and 2% twelfth graders.

Again the results were similar to the national or probability studies cited above: 97% of the girls and 70% of the boys had personally experienced sexual harassment, with most events occurring in public places. Moreover, gender differences surfaced from this survey:

> For example: 52% of the girls but only 19% of the boys were very or somewhat upset by a harassing incident; 44% of the girls surveyed worry about being sexually harassed at school, compared to 11% of the boys; and one out of three girls—but only one out of ten boys—harassed in school reported lower self-confidence as a result. (Trigg & Wittenstrom, 1996, p. 58)

The authors write: "Of the 24 categories measured by this survey, girls felt the negative impact more than boys did in 22 categories" (Trigg & Wittenstrom, 1996, p. 60).

Interesting and troubling findings about the effects on boys emerged from this study. The authors write that "boys were most disturbed by behaviors that threatened their masculinity, such as being called homosexual or being sexually harassed by other boys" (p. 59). The only harassing behavior that boys experienced at a higher rate than girls was being called gay, and boys were twice as likely to be harassed by members of their own sex (31%) than girls were by members of their sex (16%).

A limitation of this survey was that there was no mention of disabled or gay/lesbian youth.

SURVEY OF STUDENTS WITH DISABILITIES

A missing piece of the research on sexual harassment in schools is studies that look at the disabled population. A small but important pilot study of sexual harassment of students with physical disabilities was conducted by Russo with a small grant awarded to Disabilities Unlimited Consulting Services in New York City during the 1994–95 school year (Russo, 1996). Russo interviewed disabled girls and boys between the ages of 15 and 22 years old in five after-school programs and in one high school in New York City.

Focus groups and individual interviews along with a survey instrument administered to 19 girls and 7 boys provided Russo with a portrait not dissimilar to other studies on sexual harassment: Most harassers were boys; most targets were girls; and the harassment more likely occurred in front of others rather than in private settings. However, one striking finding showed that nondisabled boys were often the harassers of disabled girls, thereby throwing into question the commonly held assumption that boys in special education are often the harassers of girls.

Moreover, Russo's sample contained as many examples of adult-to-student harassment as student-to-student harassment. This disturbing finding located the adults who harassed as those unique to the special education setting: paraprofessionals/health aides or van drivers. These findings suggest that youth with disabilities may face higher rates of harassment by adults employed by the school than do their nondisabled counterparts. This finding applies both to girls as well as to boys with disabilities.

SURVEYS OF HARASSMENT OF GAY, LESBIAN, AND BISEXUAL STUDENTS

Collection of incident data on the harassment of gay, lesbian, and bisexual students is spotty and infrequent. With the exception of Massachusetts, which has a state law (Massachusetts Anti-discrimination Law, 1994) and mandated efforts that include collection of data and training programs run from the state education department, incidents of gay and lesbian harassment come to light from self-report or advocacy projects that run at the national (Gay, Lesbian, and Straight Education Network [GLSEN]) or state levels (Washington; see Reis, 1997), or from state modifications to the Youth Risk Behavior Survey (see Massachusetts Department of Education, 1998). Besides Massachusetts, Wisconsin, Connecticut, and Rhode Island have passed state laws to protect the civil rights of gay and lesbian students,[1] but no data concerning sexual harassment/violence in schools against gay/lesbian students has come yet from those states.

Gay, Lesbian, and Straight Education Network (1997)

In September 1997, GLSEN, with national offices in New York City, issued a national report card on the protection of gay and lesbian students by their schools. According to these organizations, gay and lesbian students are estimated to number around 5 million students (or 9% of the total school population). The nation's schools as a whole received a C grade, but the national average dropped to a D when Massachusetts was removed from the scoring. Massachusetts, on the other hand, received an A minus.

Among the highlights of the report's findings:

1. One half the districts reporting received a failing grade.
2. A typical high school student hears antigay slurs as often as 25.5 times a day.
3. When this occurs, only 3% of faculty will intervene in such incidences.
4. As a result of this lack of intervention, 19% of gay and lesbian students suffer physical attacks associated with sexual orientation, with 13% skipping school at least once per month and 26% dropping out all together.

The reports were based on data collected from 128 districts in 20 states nationwide and compiled by 62 GLSEN chapters. Criteria included whether schools have policies in place that protect students and teachers from harassment and discrimination, provide staff with workshops and training, provide accurate and age-appropriate information in school libraries, support extracurricular activities and clubs, and offer an accurate and inclusive curriculum.

These startling numbers, although based on self-report to an advocacy organization, when coupled with recent legal actions (see Chapter 2) taken by students against their school systems for failure to protect them from harassment, have brought attention to the discrimination, harassment, and violence suffered by gay and lesbian students.

Safe Schools Coalition (1997)

The Safe Schools Coalition is an advocacy project sponsored by dozens of organizations, including the Seattle Public Schools, the Washington Education Association, and the Seattle–King County Department of Public Health. Since January 1994, the coalition has been collecting data from people who call into a statewide toll-free hotline established to collect reports of incidents of sexual harassment or sexual violence against gay, lesbian, and bisexual individuals that have happened on school property or at school sponsored events. The project defines antigay sexual harassment as harassment on the basis of actual or perceived sexual orientation and harassment involving the use of antigay epithets.

Ninety-one incidents were reported to the hotline from January 1994 through June 1997. Targeted individuals ranged from 7 years of age through adult teachers and guest speakers. About half of the targeted individuals were male (Reis, 1997). Altogether, 75% of targeted respondents who indicated a racial identity could be described as White and 25% as people of color ("African-American" or "Black," "Black/White/Chinese," "Hispanic," "Hispanic/Creole," "Hispanic/White," "Korean/White," "Lakota," "Native American," "Native-American/Caucasian," "Indian/African-American," and "Multiracial"). Statewide, 77% of public school students are White, and 23% are people of color (Reis, 1997).

Reported incidents originated from across the state, at 59 public schools (including one Indian reservation school), at 1 private school, in 9 counties, and in 30 school districts. Eight of the school districts are mostly rural, with 1,000 to 5,000 students; 16 are midsized districts that serve suburban areas and small metropolitan areas with 5,000 to 20,000 students each; and the remaining 6 are among the largest districts in the state, serving 20,000 to more than 40,000 students each.

Reports included 8 gang rapes, 19 physical assaults (resulting in the conviction of 5 assailants), 14 incidents of physical harassment or sexual assault short of rape, 34 cases of ongoing verbal and other harassment, and a number of others involving name-calling and offensive jokes.

Since all of the incidents were self-reported, the findings cannot be generalized to other populations.

INCIDENCE OF ADULT-TO-STUDENT SEXUAL HARASSMENT IN SCHOOLS

Several of the national and state surveys on sexual harassment distinguished between sexual harassment among students and sexual harassment perpetrated by adults against students. The study based on the 1993 AAUW poll,

Hostile Hallways, found that of the 81% of students who said they were targets of sexual harassment in school, 18% were harassed by a school employee. Girls were more likely than boys to report being the target of harassment by an adult: 1 in 4 (25%) girls and 1 in 10 (10%) boys had been targeted by school employees. Distinctions by race also emerged with 33% of African-American girls reporting harassment by a school employee, as compared to 25% of white girls and 17% of Hispanic girls (AAUW, 1993).

In the Connecticut study, of the 427 students who reported receiving some unwanted sexual behaviors in school, 282 responded to the question that probed for the most upsetting incident (Permanent Commission, 1995). Of those 282, 3.5% reported that the most upsetting incident was perpetrated by a teacher, coach, or staff member.

In the study published in *Seventeen* magazine, 3.7% of the girls reported that their most serious sexual harassment experience was perpetrated by a school employee: 3% (58) cited teachers or counselors; 0.4% (8) cited school administrators; and 0.3% (7) cited other school staff. All but one of the adult harassers were male (Stein, Marshall, & Tropp, 1993).

In the Texas study, 11% of the students surveyed indicated that a school employee had perpetrated the most serious incident of sexual harassment they had experienced (Texas Civil Rights Project, 1997; see Appendix A).

THE IMPACT: EDUCATIONAL, EMOTIONAL, BEHAVIORAL

The most detailed information about the impact of sexual harassment on the lives of students comes from the AAUW study (1993). This study examined impact in three domains: educational, emotional, and behavioral; and provided the information by race and gender.

Table 1.2 shows the educational impact of sexual harassment. The most common effect was the desire to avoid school, reported by 33% of the girls and 12% of the boys. Nearly 1 in 4 girls (24%) stated that harassment prompted them to stay home or cut a class, and 32% of the girls said they did not want to talk in class. Both race and gender distinctions emerged between those who talked less in class and those who did not. Whereas 32% of the girls spoke less in class, only 13% of the boys were similarly affected. Of the African American girls, 42% indicated that they wanted to talk less in class as a result of the harassment. By comparison, 35% of the harassed Hispanic girls and 30% of the harassed white girls reported talking less (AAUW, 1993, p. 15).

The educational impact of sexual harassment also resulted in students' finding it hard to study, making a lower grade in class, thinking about changing schools, and doubting whether they had what it takes to graduate from high school.

Table 1.2. Educational Impact of Sexual Harassment

	Boys	Girls
Not wanting to go to school	12%	33%
Not wanting to talk as much in class	13%	32%
Finding it hard to pay attention in school	13%	28%
Staying home from school or cutting a class	7%	24%
Making a lower grade on a test or paper	9%	23%
Finding it hard to study	9%	22%
Making a lower grade in class	6%	20%
Thinking about changing schools	6%	18%
Doubting whether you have what it takes to graduate from high school	4%	5%

Base: the 81% of students who report some experience of sexual harassment in school

Source: Reprinted with permission from AAUW, *Hostile Hallways*, 1993, p. 15.

Students indicated the emotional impact of sexual harassment in the following ways: embarrassment, self-consciousness, being less sure of yourself, fear, doubts about being able to have a happy romantic relationship, confusion, and decreased popularity (see Table 1.3).

Finally, behavioral consequences of sexual harassment included avoiding the person (69% of the girls employed this strategy as compared with 27% of the boys), staying away from a particular place, changing seats in class, withdrawing from a particular activity or sport, changing group of friends, and changing route to/from school (see Table 1.4).

Table 1.3. Emotional Impact of Sexual Harassment

	Boys	Girls
Feeling embarrassed	36%	64%
Feeling self-conscious	21%	52%
Being less sure of yourself or less confident	14%	43%
Feeling afraid or scared	8%	39%
Doubting whether you can have a happy romantic relationship	12%	30%
Feeling confused about who you are	9%	25%
Feeling less popular	13%	18%
Feeling more popular	8%	16%

Base: the 81% of students who report some experience of sexual harassment in school

Source: Reprinted with permission from AAUW, *Hostile Hallways*, 1993, p. 16.

Table 1.4. Behavioral Impact of Sexual Harassment

	Boys	Girls
Avoiding the person who bothered/harassed you	27%	69%
Staying away from particular places in the school or on school grounds	12%	34%
Changing your seat in class to get farther away from someone	12%	31%
Stopping attending a particular activity or sport	6%	17%
Changing your group of friends	6%	14%
Changing the way you come to or go home from school	6%	14%
Base: the 81% of students who report some experience of sexual harassment in school		

Source: Reprinted with permission from AAUW, *Hostile Hallways*, 1993, p. 18.

CONCLUSIONS FROM THE SURVEYS

Students, whether they are the targets, witnesses, or perpetrators of harassment, overwhelmingly acknowledge the existence of sexual harassment in schools. There is no shortage of evidence pointing toward a firm conclusion that sexual harassment in schools is rampant, and that the targets are not passive in the face of this harassment.

Yet, despite all the cumulative evidence from these studies, both those with probability/scientific methodologies (samples culled from the entire country and from the state of Connecticut) as well as from the studies that have only looked at one school or one state or employed less than scientific methods, there seems to be a continuing compulsion to survey the phenomenon and existence of sexual harassment.

It is safe to assume at this point that we can believe the results, which amounts to believing the students. It is time to expand survey research to include either longitudinal studies that would follow cohorts of students or to invest in outcome/effectiveness studies that would focus on a spectrum of interventions to reduce and prevent sexual harassment. Moreover, as I will argue in Chapter 7 of this book, we need to readminister sexual harassment surveys to inquire about the nature of the relationship between the harasser and the target(s) because in many instances theirs is not an anonymous relationship but rather one of familiarity and even intimacy.

On the other hand, the statistics that have emerged from these surveys and research studies might have dropped quickly into oblivion, or at least been taken less seriously, were it not for the complaints and lawsuits that girls and young women, and in rare instances, boys, have been filing, and winning, in state and federal courts in the past decade. The next chapter will take us through some of those lawsuits and complaints.

179027

2

Lawsuits and Complaints: New Sources of Evidence of Sexual Harassment in Schools

EVEN THOUGH a lawsuit is a sample size of one, there may be nothing atypical about a single lawsuit. In fact, lawsuits may be prototypical and serve as guideposts for future directions. Maybe it is time for social scientists and educators who are interested in documenting the problem of sexual harassment in schools to regard lawsuits as a new form of evidence and as material that holds valuable lessons.

A summary of the major federal lawsuits and complaints filed through the Office for Civil Rights of the U.S. Department of Education has produced evidence that documents the impact of sexual harassment on the lives of the targets. Among the consequences of sexual harassment that have been stipulated through lawsuits are absenteeism; dropping out of a particular class or school; lower grades; sleeplessness and physical symptoms/complaints; fear of separation from adults, be they parents or school personnel (i.e., refusal to take the school bus, refusal to participate in recess, asking to stay in the classroom or be sent to the principal's or nurse's office during recess, refusal to eat lunch in the cafeteria and choosing to stay in the classroom or library during lunch); depression; weight loss/gain; and threats to commit suicide. Students also expressed a reduction of trust toward adults and in their belief that school is a safe and fair environment; they felt betrayed, trivialized, and dismissed if and when they told school personnel about the incidents of sexual harassment that they had experienced. These lessons may linger far beyond the actual episodes of the sexual harassment: trust of adults erode, school is a place to be avoided, and justice is not delivered.

Granted, some of this evidence gleaned from lawsuits is biased in that it is provided by the plaintiff or the experts who have been hired by the plaintiff's attorney. On the other hand, the opposing counsel's grueling interrogation of the plaintiff (especially in the discovery/deposition phase of the case when there is no judge or jury present) makes the process of proceeding with a lawsuit very difficult and leaves the pursuit of lawsuits to those plaintiffs and their parents who are particularly zealous and motivated. Thus, lawsuits may or may not be typical. Even so, there are many lessons to be learned that might spare others from heading in the same direction in the future. To that extent, we should not dismiss the information that can be derived from the lawsuits whether these cases are won, lost, or settled out of court.

LANDMARK DECISION: THE *FRANKLIN* CASE

It takes only one influential lawsuit to change the landscape and discourse. Such a sea change occurred with the February 1992 landmark 9-to-0 decision of the U.S. Supreme Court in the *Franklin v. Gwinnett County (GA) Public Schools* case, bringing accelerated attention from school administrators to the problem of sexual harassment and sex discrimination in schools, and establishing the right to sue for compensatory damages under Title IX. For the first time in the 20-year existence of Title IX, the federal law that guarantees an educational environment free from sex discrimination and, by implication and interpretation, sexual harassment, schools could be held liable for compensatory damages if they failed to provide an educational environment that was free from sex discrimination.

The facts of *Franklin* case revolve around a 15-year-old young woman who had sex, three times, with a teacher on school grounds. When she reported it, first to a teacher whom she trusted and then to the school administrators, they told her not to tell anyone—not her parents, not the police, not her boyfriend—and that they would get rid of the offending teacher. The teacher agreed to resign and the school agreed to drop all matters pending against him. The plaintiff, Christine Franklin, won on the grounds that the school had discriminated against her on the basis of sex, and the Supreme Court for the first time allowed compensatory damages for such a plaintiff.

Beyond the power and precedent that one lawsuit can establish, narratives and anecdotal information from girls and young women parallel the experiences of sexual harassment in schools that are documented in the lawsuits and complaints. In other words, in terms of content, there is nothing atypical about the lawsuits (Lawton, 1993, 1996; Lewin, 1994, 1995; Stein, 1995a).

PROTOTYPICAL LAWSUITS:
ECHOING THE THEMES FROM THE SURVEYS

In each of the lawsuits and complaints discussed in depth in this section, the three main themes that emerged from the *Seventeen* study (Stein, Marshall, & Tropp, 1993)—the public nature of sexual harassment, the nonpassive (i.e., active) responses of the targets, and the denial or trivialization by school officials—are echoed. Almost without exception, each incident of sexual harassment outlined in the lawsuits or complaints took place in public; the targets were not passive—they either stood up to the harasser, or told someone; and without exception, the school officials trivialized and minimized the incident or denied that sexual harassment took place. Whether the targets or perpetrators were male or female, and regardless of their age (age 6 through late teens), with or without the involvement of their parents, school officials typically issued denials about the presence of sexual harassment in their buildings.

Of the nearly two dozen salient cases discussed in this section, seven emanated from boys whose harassment came from other boys (one in elementary school, one in middle school, and five in high school). There are a total of five cases involving elementary school students (four girls and one boy), five cases from middle school (four girls and one boy), and twelve from high school (five of which involve boys as plaintiffs, and two cases that involved same-sex, girl-to-girl harassment). Only one of these 22 cases involve conduct that happened in a private setting, without bystanders. All but one of these cases had only one plaintiff at a time; the exception was one case that involved a group of high school girls who initiated joint litigation and won in an out-of-court settlement (*Krengel v. Santa Clara Unified School District*, 1997). However, this unusual case is not atypical in one respect: Like many other lawsuits, it was settled out of court, a condition that often imposes restrictions of confidentiality upon the parties. Although out-of-court settlements spare the parties a lengthy, expensive legal process, these agreements also serve to deny the public, including researchers and journalists, access to all the lessons that may be derived from a particular case so that other school officials need not repeat the same mistakes.

As we embark on this journey through lawsuits, be prepared for contradictions. Sometimes the outcomes of the various cases make it seem that we in the United States are divided into different countries: The same set of facts in one part of the country render a decision in one direction from a federal court, whereas in a different part of the country a similar set of facts leads a federal court in the opposite decision. In other instances, the Office for Civil Rights (OCR) of the U.S. Department of Education, the federal agency charged with investigating sexual harassment complaints, will find in one direction whereas the state agency that is charged with investigating discrimination issues a totally opposite decision. Rather than being dismissed as a classic case of the left hand not knowing what the right hand is doing, these inconsistencies seem to be examples of our society attempting to make law about new problems.

In one case that is often cited in popular magazines and teen literature and on television talk and news shows, Katy Lyle, a 15-year-old at Duluth Central High School in Duluth, Minnesota, was targeted through nasty graffiti that covered the walls of one stall in the boys' bathroom on the third floor of the high school (*Lyle v. Independent School District #709*, 1991). The statements included "Katy does it with farm animals," "Katy is a slut," "Katy gives good head," and "Katy sucked my dick after she sucked my dog's dick." Additionally, boys would yell out across the hallways, "Hey, Katy, I took a leak in your stall today," and girls would wonder aloud what Katy had done to "deserve" this (interviews with Carol and Katy Lyle conducted by Katie Couric, *The Today Show*, October 7, 1992). Katy was tormented daily on the school bus and as she entered the school (LeBlanc, 1992).

Despite repeated requests from Katy and her parents to the principal to have the graffiti removed, it remained on the walls for a period of 16 months. The principal's responses included "No one reads it anyhow" and "It'll make you a stronger person." He also claimed that his hands were tied by the custodians' union contract, which only made provision for the walls to be repainted once every 2 years and since they had just completed a painting assignment, they could not paint over that graffiti. Finally, her older brother, home from college during a vacation, removed the graffiti in a matter of minutes. Although the physical evidence was removed, the taunting continued.

In a 1991 settlement with the Minnesota Department of Human Rights, Katy and her family were awarded $15,000, and the school district agreed to implement training programs for staff and students to develop and disseminate a sexual harassment policy. They also agreed to appoint an administrator to coordinate these efforts.

Another widely publicized case from Minnesota (*Mutziger v. Independent School District #272*, 1992; also cited as *Eden Prairie School District #272*, 1993) involved the youngest child to file a sexual harassment complaint. In this case, both the Minnesota Department of Human Rights and the Office for Civil Rights (OCR) of the U.S. Department of Education found that a 6-year-old girl named Cheltzie Hentz (and eventually several other girls) had been sexually harassed on the bus, on the school grounds, and in the classroom by boys who ranged in age from 6 through 13 years. The perpetrators were accused of making lewd remarks and sexual taunts, including references about girls' body parts and explicit suggestions about her having oral sex with her father.

This case became notable for the age of the target and the age of the perpetrators; Cheltzie was and remains the youngest child to file and win a sexual harassment complaint. In the stunning decision rendered by OCR, the "reasonable woman standard" was invoked to apply to 6-year-old children[1]:

> From the standpoint of a reasonable female student participating in district programs and activities . . . , the sexually offensive conduct was sufficiently frequent, severe, and/or protracted to impair significantly the educational services and benefits offered. . . . In this case, there is no question that even the youngest girls understood that the language and conduct being used were expressions of hostility toward them on the basis of their sex and, as a clear result, were offended and upset. (*Eden Prairie*, 1993, p. 12)

In Cheltzie's case, all of the events occurred around adults—either the bus driver or bus monitors, or in the case of classroom incidences, in the presence of the classroom teacher. As part of the investigation, other girls were interviewed about the same boys who were accused of harassing Cheltzie. According to the OCR finding:

> During a social studies class, a seventh grade male student repeatedly made remarks of a sexual nature . . . touched the girls, and on one occasion, physically restrained one of them so that she could not escape his lewd remarks. According to the female students, the teacher witnessed the harassment, but was unresponsive to their requests for assistance. The teacher's response was to offer to change the boy's seat. According to the students, the boy's seat already had been changed numerous times as girls reported that he was bothering them. (p. 9)

Again, adults watched, students appealed for help, and adults offered innocuous and insipid solutions.

The behavior of school personnel is mentioned in most federal lawsuits. For example, in a 1992 lawsuit in federal district court in Connecticut, Johana Mennone, a student at Amity Regional High School in Woodbridge, Connecticut, alleged that "in the presence of her teacher and a roomful of classmates, a male student grabbed her hair, legs, breasts, and buttocks nearly every day. He repeatedly made remarks about her breasts and told her that he was going to rape her" (Lawton, 1993). Again, a teacher watched while outright assaults took place in the classroom. In a June 15, 1995, ruling in federal district court, Judge Gerald L. Goettel ruled that school personnel could be held liable for failing to prevent sexual harassment between students (*Mennone v. Gordon*, 1995). Along with another case in Connecticut with similar facts, but with middle school students as the protagonists and plaintiff (*Stern v. Milford*, 1993), settlements were reached out of court in 1996, in favor of the plaintiffs.

A most unusual case emerged in Santa Clara, California, unique not for the particulars of the allegations against the high school boys and the school officials, but because the girls involved acted collectively in their outrage, and ultimately shared in their victory. The case, known as the Teddie Bears (*Krengel v. Santa Clara Unified School District*, 1997), entered popular (teenage) culture largely because it was the subject of a made-for-television film, *Stand Against Fear* (Schneder & Jeffery, 1996), and an article in *Seventeen* magazine (Ratcliffe, 1996).

The Teddie Bears, an 18-year tradition at Santa Clara High School, was an all-female sports club whose members attended all the varsity football games and compiled statistics for the players. The girls alleged sexual harassment, verbal insults, and assault by the football players. Beginning in October 1995, the girls began a process of reporting the sexual harassment incidents to the football coach, vice principal, principal, superintendent, and school board. After being told by the principal that he could not assure their safety, the 15-member squad resigned en masse.

With the exception of three boys who were suspended for the creation and distribution of a "slam book" (a handmade book filled with sexually degrading pictures of girls accompanied by vulgar written comments), the other harassers were not disciplined (Gaura, 1996). Interestingly, the school did not take any disciplinary actions against the harassers until some of the girls had filed a civil lawsuit. This case not only typifies the denial of sexual harassment in schools, but also the privileging of male athletes in high schools (Benedict, 1997; Lefkowitz, 1997).

Prior to taking legal action, the parents of the girls had taken their complaints to the Santa Clara District Attorney's office, hoping to pursue the matter as a criminal complaint (Gaura, 1996). That route proved futile. However, with the added weight of the intervention of the U.S. Justice Department, the case was settled out of court. The terms of the settlement are confidential, but money did exchange hands (Gaura, 1997). The Teddie Bear sports club has not been revived since the 15 girls resigned in October 1995.

On the other hand, in the middle of Iowa, two cases (*Burrow v. Postville Community School District*, 1996; and *Wright v. Mason City School District*, 1996) were filed as Title IX violations (Fuson, 1994). In the case of Lisa Burrow, tried in a U.S. district court, the jury found that the school was not liable for the harassment.

In the *Wright* case, the federal court judge set aside the decision of the jury. The jury had heard the case that alleged peer sexual harassment and in June 1996 awarded Heather Wright, the plaintiff in the case, an award of $5,200 plus all attorney's fees. The jury had concluded that a hostile environment of peer sexual harassment existed and that the school district had failed to protect her from it (Simbro, 1996). In a rather stunning turn of events, U.S. federal judge John Jarvey reversed the decision of the jury, ruling that victims of student-to-student harassment must show that the school not only knew about the harassment but also intentionally did nothing to stop it ("Student Failed to Show School District's Intent to Discriminate in Peer Sexual Harassment Case," 1997). Furthermore, the judge stated in his opinion an appeal for clarity from Congress:

> Given the enormous social implications for students, school and parents, this court wishes that Congress would step in and simply tell us whether it intended to make school districts responsible for the payment of damages to students under these circumstances. . . . Knowing that that will not occur, the court [has done] its best to decipher congressional intent. ("Iowa Judge Overturns Jury Verdict for Victim," 1996, p. 4)

Compounding the lack of clarity that the federal court judge in Iowa articulated, contradictory rulings have emerged from different federal court jurisdictions, thereby adding to the confusion about peer-to-peer sexual harassment. Three U.S. courts of appeals (the Second, Fifth, and Eleventh Circuits) have issued similar opinions, yet their decisions disagree with opinions that have come from two others (the Seventh and Ninth Circuits).

U.S. COURTS OF APPEALS OPINIONS:
THE SECOND, FIFTH, AND ELEVENTH CIRCUITS
VS. THE SEVENTH AND NINTH CIRCUITS

The U.S. courts of appeals are finally locked in a disagreement; the Second, Fifth, and Eleventh Circuits are in disagreement with the Seventh and the Ninth.

Eleventh Circuit

In a Georgia case, *Davis. v. Monroe County (GA) Board of Education* (1994), U.S. district court judge Wilbur D. Owens, Jr., of Macon, Georgia, ruled on August 29, 1994, that the school district was not liable for a fifth-grade student's alleged harassment of another student. He dismissed the case on the grounds that the school did not have a special custodial relationship with its students and had no special duty to protect them from other students (Walsh, 1994). The complainant had alleged that school officials were slow to react to the harassing conduct by a boy who repeatedly tried to touch a girl's breasts, rubbed his body against hers, and used vulgar language.

Yet, on February 14, 1996, the district court's decision was overturned by the Eleventh Circuit. The appeal was argued by Verna Williams, senior counsel with the National Women's Law Center, on August 30, 1995. An Eleventh Circuit panel, in a 2-to-1 decision, overturned Judge Owens's decision, and sent the case back to him for trial. Writing for the majority, Judge Rosemary Barkett wrote: "A female student should not be required to run a gauntlet of sexual abuse in return for the privilege of being allowed to obtain an education" (*Davis v. Monroe Country Board of Education*, 1996). However, the school district appealed the decision, and the decision was vacated, pending a rehearing on October 23, 1996, before the full Eleventh Circuit court.

On August 21, 1997, the full Eleventh Circuit court issued a decision in the *Davis* case. In a 7 to 4 decision, the court asserted that school districts are not liable for failing to stop student-to-student sexual harassment. This decision applies only to schools in the Eleventh Circuit, which covers Florida, Georgia, and Alabama, and agrees with decisions from the Fifth Circuit, which covers Texas, Louisiana, and Oklahoma. However, the majority noted that 10 district courts have ruled to the contrary—that schools can in fact be held liable for peer harassment. This case was heard by the U.S. Supreme Court in January 1999 as the first peer-to-peer sexual harassment case to go before the high court (Stein, 1999). A decision will be announced before the end of the term in June 1999 (see Epilogue).

Fifth Circuit

In agreement with the Eleventh Circuit was an opinion issued in April 1996 by the Fifth Circuit. In *Rowinsky v. Bryan (TX) Independent School District*, two sisters who had been eighth-grade students claimed that they had been tormented throughout the 1992–93 school year by a boy on their school bus who had grabbed at their breasts and genitals and who used foul and lewd language (Walsh, 1996b). The girls' parents complained regularly to school officials. However, the U.S. district court dismissed the original lawsuit, and the U.S. court of appeals, in a 2-to-1 decision, upheld that decision, saying that the girls had no claim under Title IX because the harassment was not conducted by school employees.

Second Circuit

On November 15, 1994, Thomas J. McAvoy, chief federal court judge for the Northern District of New York in Albany, issued a ruling that held teachers and administrators liable and responsible for preventing student-to-student sexual harassment in schools. In this case, *Bruneau v. South Kortright (NY) Central School District* (1996), the court ruled that a sixth-grade girl who was taunted with sexual comments ("prostitute," "dog-faced bitch," and "lesbo") and physically abused by boys in her class could sue her teacher and an assistant superintendent under 42 U.S.C. Section 1983 (of the Civil Rights Act of 1871).[2] She was also able to bring a suit against the school district under Title IX and recover compensatory damages, punitive damages, and attorney fees. The school district was found liable in the New York case because teachers and administrators were alerted to the assaults but took no action. In fact, when the girl's parents complained of the abusive behavior to their daughter's teacher, they were told that "the boys would be all over her in a few years" (Jones, 1994, p. 12). The parents requested assistance from the assistant superintendent of the school district following this meeting with the teacher, but again, no attempts to remedy the situation were made. When the parents asked that their daughter be allowed to transfer to another class, their request was denied. At that point, the girl transferred to another school and the parents took legal action. The judge's ruling in this case provides that a plaintiff can proceed against a school district if the district's inaction (or insufficient action) in response to complaints of student-to-student sexual harassment is the result of an actual intent to discriminate against the student on the basis of sex.

However, when the *Bruneau* case finally was tried before a jury in November 1996, the jury found in favor of the school district, and against the teenage girl. In a ruling issued on December 31, 1998, the U.S. Court of Appeals for the Second Circuit upheld the decision of the district court (*Bruneau v. South Kortright Central School District*, 1998).

Ninth Circuit

However, in the Ninth Circuit, which covers California, Oregon, Washington, and Alaska, a totally different standard of liability emerged. In *Oona v. McCaffrey*, the court ruled that administrators can be held individually responsible for failing to stop sexual harassment. This stunning decision strips government officials of qualified immunity when they violate constitutional rights. Quoting from the opinion, the court said: "A school official in a supervisory position cannot claim immunity for the failure to respond to complaints of harassment" ("Court Carves New Path in Sexual Harassment Cases," 1997, pp. 3–4).

This case arises from a lawsuit against the Santa Rosa, California, school district brought by the parents of a sixth-grade girl who sued her teacher, the principal, and the director of elementary education because they failed to remove a student teacher from the classroom after he had been accused of fondling their daughter in class and lowering her grades after she complained.

In addition, their lawsuit claimed that the school district is liable for failing to prevent other students from sexually harassing the girl. The harassment from the other students included subjecting the sixth-grade girl to hostile comments: Her body parts were referred to as "melons" and "beaver," and she and other girls in the class were called slang terms for prostitute ("Suit Proceeds Against Individual Officials for Failing to Stop Sexual Harassment," 1997). Moreover, one male student hit Oona in the face and told her to "get used to it." The school district knew of the harassment emanating from both the student teacher and the other students, and had failed to prevent this behavior; and these "are sufficient to show violations of clearly established Title IX rights" ("Suit Proceeds Against Individual Officials for Failing to Stop Sexual Harassment," 1997, p. 5).

Seventh Circuit

On March 3, 1998, a decision was issued by the Seventh Circuit about a young woman who had been subjected to ongoing peer sexual harassment by a group of boys in her public high school sponsored by the University of Illinois (*Jane Doe v. University of Illinois*, 1998). The court did not rule on the sufficiency of her allegations of sexual harassment (pp. 2–3) but rather on the standard of liability for the school personnel. They held that schools have an obligation to intervene when they have actual knowledge, and that failing to take action will incur liability. Moreover, the Seventh Circuit refused to rehear the case en banc (meaning that all the judges would hear the case, and not just a panel of three), thus making their ruling stand as law for all states in the Seventh Circuit (Illinois, Indiana, and Wisconsin).

DISTRICT COURT DECISIONS

These forceful decisions from the Seventh and Ninth Circuits are in opposition to the decisions rendered by the Second, Fifth, and Eleventh Circuits and will necessitate clarification from the Supreme Court. In the meantime, contradictory decisions are free to reign in other circuits, applying totally different applications and interpretations of Title IX and sexual harassment law to the schools. In fact, it is not uncommon for U.S. district court judges to mention that their U.S. court of appeals has yet to rule on the matter and provide them with guidance ("Court Rules New Hampshire School District May Be Liable Under Title IX for Failing to Curtail Peer Harassment," 1997). Echoing the federal district court judge in Iowa who asked for clarity from Congress, other U.S. district court judges, it seems, are asking not only the U.S. courts of appeals but also the Supreme Court for clarification.

BOY-TO-BOY SEXUAL HARASSMENT CASES

In October 1994 in Utah, the U.S. federal district court refused to allow a locker room incident, directed at one football player by his fellow teammates, as an actionable case of hostile-environment sexual harassment. In Judge Benson's decision, the lawsuit against the Sky View High School and the Cache County (UT) School District was dismissed on the grounds that the boy failed to prove that he had been a victim of any concerted discriminatory effort (*Seamons v. Snow,* 1994).

In the fall of 1993, after a football game, the young man, Brian Seamons, was restrained by four of his teammates and painfully taped naked to a towel rack after he left the shower area. He was further humiliated when a girl was involuntarily dragged in to view him (Brown, 1995; "Court Dismisses Male Student's Title IX Harassment Claim," 1994). Brian claimed that this traditional team ritual imposed on any player who moved from second string to first string was well known to the coach and to school officials.

The school authorities continued either to excuse the behavior as gender appropriate (i.e., "boys will be boys") or merely a case of team hazing; Brian was blamed for bringing the incident to public's attention. The football coach reacted to Brian's complaints by first suspending and then dismissing him from the football team. The next day, the superintendent canceled the remaining football games, prompting the coach, Douglas Snow, to demand that Brian apologize to the team for this cause of action. Neither Snow nor any of the football players were disciplined for their behaviors in this incident. In fact, Snow stated publicly that "it was inappropriate to impose discipline on the other players for hazing" ("Hazing or Sexual Harassment? Football Player Appeals Ruling," 1995, p. 5). Sadly, retaliation against both Brian and his family caused him to transfer to a different school district (Stein, 1995a).

Brian and his family filed a Title IX sex discrimination case against the school district. However, the judge found no fault on the part of the coach or school administrators. In part, the decision read:

> It may have been wrong, or right, or ethical, or unethical, or noble, or ignoble, but no plausible treatment theory could construe it as an act intended to treat

Brian negatively because he is a boy. . . . Because plaintiffs have not alleged that defendants' conduct was sexual in any way . . . [the] allegations are not sufficient to base a claim of sexual harassment. (*Seamons v. Snow*, 1994, p. 1118)

Notwithstanding the narrow basis upon which the judge decided to interpret the claim of sex discrimination, the judge might have offered some moral guidance from the bench, as judges often do.

Moreover, educators may be left wondering if the gender of the participants had any bearing on the outcome of this case, from the origin of this ritual in the locker room to the decision rendered in the courtroom. The question remains for educators, if not for judges: Why should the gender of the target make any difference when the behavior is publicly performed, seemingly school-approved, gendered violence (Stein, 1995b)?

In an appeal to this decision, the Tenth Circuit upheld the dismissal of the sexual harassment, Title IX claim, but ruled that the lower court had erred in dismissing Brian's First Amendment claim. Seamons and his parents had alleged that their freedom of speech had been violated when school officials had discouraged them for making statements to the press and had removed Brian from the football team when he refused to apologize for having informed authorities of the incident ("Administrators' Handling of Athlete's 'Hazing' Did Not Violate Title IX, 10th Circuit Says," 1996). It is worth noting that in one of the opinions, Judge Monroe McKay expressed doubt that the incident wasn't sexual in nature: "It is hard for me to believe that the display of the male genitalia to a female for other than medical or educational reasons has a non-sexual connotation" ("School's Reaction to Hazing Raises Free Speech Issues," 1996, p. 6).

Besides the Utah case, and around the same time, in yet another part of the country, an 11-year-old boy was undergoing harassment from fellow middle school students. John B., in Orland, California, was harassed and assaulted at first by eighth-grade boys off of school grounds, but then regularly on school grounds by a group of boys and a few girls. His parents complained regularly to the principal, but over the course of the year of John's torment, that middle school had three different principals, and each one offered one ineffective solution after another, each abrogating to John the responsibility for ending the harassment. All of the principals' suggestions required changes in John's conduct, rather than changes in the conduct of the harassers: They made suggestions that he study self-defense and that he avoid the tormentors; and a final one hinted that if the principal were to call the tormentors into the office, the harassment would only get worse. In the words of John's therapist, John was "suffering from nightmares, fearfulness, increased isolation and diminished ability to cope" (Seligman, 1996, p. A16).

Left with no other option, in the fall of 1994, John's parents hired an attorney, who filed a Title IX action in the federal court (*John B. v. Orland Joint Union School District*, 1996). However, in July 1996, an out-of-court settlement was reached, awarding John $55,000, and no admission of wrongdoing on the part of the school district. In the meantime, like Brian Seamons in Utah, John moved to a different school district.

There are no other boy-to-boy sexual harassment cases that have been filed in federal court (see the following section for discussion of an OCR complaint filed in Minnesota).

LITIGATION ON BEHALF OF GAY STUDENTS

A landmark decision was rendered in November 1996 by an unanimous jury in a federal court case that found three school district administrators had violated the rights of a gay young man. The following day, in an out-of-court settlement, the Ashland, Wisconsin, school district agreed to award Jamie Nabozny, a former student, a $900,000 award for the harassment that he endured for more than 4 years on school grounds (Terry, 1996; Walsh, 1996a), with $62,000 additional funds awarded for medical expenses (*Nabozny v. Podlesny*, 1996).

This case is shocking not merely for the torment that was inflicted on school grounds upon the young man, but also for the egregious negligence demonstrated by the school officials. From 7th grade through 11th grade, when Nabozny dropped out of high school, while he was subjected to violent acts of hostility based on his sexual identity (acts that included being urinated on and being assaulted by other boys who held him down while simulating a rape), school officials mishandled or totally ignored his requests for help and intervention. One principal repeatedly promised to act on his complaints, yet also claimed that Nabozny should get used to these behaviors since he was so openly gay while another administrator allegedly said that Nabozny deserved this behavior ("School District Reaches Settlement with Former Student for Over $900,000," 1997).

His case is the first of its kind for a gay or lesbian student, and is also significant because the equal protection clause of the Fourteenth Amendment (42 U.S.C. §1983) was used for the first time in a case involving a gay or lesbian student. Although frequently used in sexual harassment cases when school personnel have been sexually involved with a minor student, thus incurring liability upon the school administrators for failure to act, supervise, or protect the minor student, never before had this law been applied to the equal protection of gay and lesbian students.

Another case that involved a gay young man was settled for far less money and no acknowledgment of liability on the part of the school district. However, the case, known as *Doe v. Riverside-Brookfield High School District*, did involve a financial settlement to cover Mario Doe's expenses for counseling, tutorial, and educational services (Walsh, 1997a).

A case against the Kent, Washington, school district was filed by Mark Iversen. A graduated senior from Kentwood High School, Mark Iversen alleged that the school failed to protect him from the antigay verbal and physical harassment of other students. Harassed from the 7th grade through the 12th grade in three separate Kent schools, Mark was frequently called a "faggot," "queer," and "homo," had his life threatened on several occasions, and in perhaps the most shocking incident, was severely beaten in his classroom by eight students. Similar to the *Nabozny* case, administrators allegedly told Mark (prior to the severe beating) that he had brought the harassment on himself and should expect such abuse if he acted gay (Reis, 1997).

Represented by the ACLU, Iversen in his lawsuit also claimed that the school's failure to stop the harassment violated Mark's equal protection under the Fourteenth Amendment. The lawsuit was settled on November 6, 1998, with the Kent School District agreeing to pay $40,000 and educate teachers and administrators about peer sexual harassment based on sexual orientation (Walsh, 1998b).

More litigation on behalf of gay and lesbian students will no doubt emerge in the future (Ruenzel, 1999).

ADULT-TO-STUDENT SEXUAL HARASSMENT CASES

There are many cases that have traveled through federal courts both at the district and circuit court levels seeking redress for incidences of adult-to-student sexual harassment, using Section 1983 of the Equal Protection Clause of the Fourteenth Amendment, plus federal law Title IX, as avenues of redress. The decisions are as contradictory as they are plentiful and varied. In large part, decisions in the Fifth Circuit (*Jane Doe v. Taylor Independent School District*, 1994), and a recent one in the Eleventh Circuit (*Floyd v. Waiters*, 1998) have been in favor of the school district (and their employees), whereas decisions in other parts of the country have often held for the aggrieved students (in the Third Circuit, *Stoneking v. Bradford Area School District* in 1989; *J.O., P.O. v. Alton Community School District* in December 1992 in the Seventh Circuit; and several cases discussed previously from the Ninth Circuit). Since there are many cases that are usually in flux at any given time it is difficult to draw generalizations from them, and therefore discussion of these cases have been omitted from this book.

However, the U.S. Supreme Court heard a case on March 25, 1998 that involved sexual harassment and a sexual relationship between a student and a teacher (*Gebser v. Lago Vista Independent School District*, also known as *Doe v. Lago Vista Independent School District*, 1997; "Supreme Court to Hear Harassment Case Stemming from Teacher-Student Relationship," 1998). The case involved a ninth-grade girl who had sexual relations with a teacher for more than a year; she never told school officials or her parents. The relationship only came to light when a policeman discovered them in a parked car. The teacher was dismissed and was criminally prosecuted (Greenhouse, 1998).

On June 22, 1998, the Supreme Court issued its deeply divided, 5-to-4 decision on this case. The high court's split decision ruled that districts can only be held liable under Title IX if school officials in a position of authority were informed of the misconduct and then failed to act. This highly restrictive standard is even above the liability standard set for employers under Title VII. ("Good News for Schools: Supreme Court Limits Liability for Teacher-Student Harassment," 1998; Greenberger & Williams, 1998). Writing for the majority, Justice Sandra Day O'Connor stated that victims of sexual harassment cannot collect monetary damages under Title IX (as the *Franklin* case had established) unless "an official who, at a minimum, has authority to address the alleged discrimination and to institute corrective measures . . . has actual knowledge of discrimination and fails adequately to respond" (Walsh, 1998a, p. 30).

However, Justice John Paul Stevens, writing for the dissent, said that the Court's majority "ranks the protection of the school district's purse above protection of immature high school students" ("Opinions in sexual harassment case," 1998, p. 31). This decision is also a rejection of the Department of Education's interpretation of Title IX, which claimed that "a school district could be found liable, regardless of whether officials knew of the misconduct, if a teacher had misused his position of authority in carrying out the harassment" (Greenhouse, 1998).

No doubt this case and the *Franklin* case will be compared and debated among lawyers and generally cause confusion among educators for quite some time.

CONCLUSION FROM THE LAWSUITS

If this lengthy trip through legal decisions has left the reader confused, imagine the plight of the plaintiffs, and all the time, effort, and money that they and their families expend. In many instances, cases drag out for 5 to 7 years, traveling through various attorneys and courtrooms; children grow up, move on, and graduate before some of these cases are resolved.

A totally different route of adjudication is available to aggrieved individuals through the Office for Civil Rights of the U.S. Department of Education. The supposed benefits of this route, as opposed to filing a lawsuit in federal court, are the allegedly speedy time lines for investigations, and the fact that one does not need an attorney. It is to that route that we now turn our attention.

COMPLAINTS FILED WITH THE U.S. DEPARTMENT OF EDUCATION, OFFICE FOR CIVIL RIGHTS

Despite troubling and contradictory rulings from federal court, students continue to file Title IX complaints with OCR. In 1991, 11 complaints were filed against the school districts; in 1995, that number had risen to 80, in 1997 to 125, and in 1998 to 102. Although OCR cannot award compensatory damages to an aggrieved individual, they can compel the school district to pay for costs incurred from counseling, tutoring, transportation, and tuition for the complainant. They can also require the district to provide training for staff and students on the subjects of sex discrimination and sexual harassment (Pitsch, 1994b). Among the hundreds of districts that OCR has investigated, letters of findings (LOFs) or settlement agreements, or both, have been issued to school districts in Millis, Massachusetts; Petaluma, California; Meridian, Texas; Washoe County School District, Reno, Nevada; Sweet Home, Oregon; Mason City, Iowa; Albion, Michigan; Fayetteville, Arkansas; and Victor Valley Union High School District, Victorville, California.[3]

Same-Sex Sexual Harassment (Girl to Girl)

Notable among OCR's letters of findings are two in which the sexual harassment incidents involved students of the same sex. Both complaints involved high school girls who sexually harassed other girls, one case from San Jose, California (*East Side Union High School District*, 1993), and the other from Bolton, Massachusetts (*Nashoba Regional School District*, 1993). The facts in both cases are strikingly similar: A single girl at each site was subjected to verbal and written sexual harassment over a period of many months. The harassment consisted of sexually explicit taunts, graffiti, and rumors of the girl's alleged sexual behavior with male students. Both young women saw their grades fall; one cut classes and altered her walking route to avoid further harassment (San Jose), and the other required private counseling (Bolton). In both cases, school officials had been informed of the harassment, yet they failed to treat it as such.

In the Massachusetts case, the school personnel claimed that the girl was writing the graffiti about herself or inventing it. The school officials wanted to go as far as to get a handwriting analysis before they would believe her. According to the letter of finding from OCR in the Massachusetts case,

The student evidenced an extensive record of her numerous and repeated efforts to end the conduct. The student immediately reported the graffiti to her counselor upon discovering it in the bathroom. On her own initiative, the student weekly, and sometimes daily, reported new graffiti to the principal or her counselor, and she kept detailed notes of verbal harassment incidences. The student herself removed some of the graffiti from the bathrooms and walls. (*Nashoba*, 1993, p. 9)

The response and rationale from the San Jose, California, school staff was to assume that sexual harassment could only occur "when a student approaches another student of the opposite sex and makes lewd gestures or asks for sexual favors" (*East Side Union High School District*, 1993, p. 5). Moreover, they did not consider the conduct between members of the same sex to be possible sexual harassment, especially since the target and her harassers had once been friends. For all of these reasons, the school district did not investigate the complaint.

In both of these complaints, OCR concluded that there had been pervasive, persistent, and severe sexual harassment in violation of Title IX, and that the school districts had inadequate grievance procedures for prompt and equitable resolution of complaints of sexual harassment.

Elementary School–Based Cases of Sexual Harassment

Despite sharp rulings in these two same sex cases, another regional office of OCR refused to investigate a Minnesota third-grade student's claim that he was sexually harassed by other boys at school for several months. Jonathan Harms of the Sauk Rapids–Rice School district, who documented his verbal harassment on a small, concealed tape recorder, was sexually taunted over a period of months by about a dozen of his male classmates in the third grade. The harassment escalated to an assault when his pants and underwear were pulled down to below his knees. Yet, OCR responded in June 1993 to the parent's complaint by stating that it found "no indication that the student was singled out for harassment because of his sex" (*Sauk Rapids-Rice*, 1993).

Protests about OCR's decision came from both expected and unexpected quarters. Jonathan's parents responded by saying that "their son's case sends a 'disturbing' message: while girls are protected from the sexual taunts of their male peers, boys are not" (Brown, 1994a, p. 1). Minnesota Attorney General Hubert H. Humphrey, III, sent a letter on January 6, 1994, to U.S. Secretary of Education Richard Riley, seeking an explanation for OCR's decision not to investigate: "I would appreciate clarification of whether boys are covered under Title IX. I ask that the OCR reconsider its decision not to investigate the . . . case" (Brown, 1994a, p. 2). In an October 17, 1994, letter to Senator

Durenberger of Minnesota, Norma Cantu, the assistant secretary for civil rights of the U.S. Department of Education's Office for Civil Rights, indicated that the investigation might be reopened (Pitsch, 1994a). This turn of events was undoubtedly influenced by the Minnesota Department of Human Rights' September 1994 decision that found "probable cause" in the *Harms* case; the department has decided to investigate Jonathan's claim as sexual harassment under state law (*Harms v. Independent School District #47*, 1993).

Two California cases (*Modesto City Schools*, 1993; *Newark Unified School District*, 1993) investigated by the Office for Civil Rights provide sharp contrast to the outcome in the Jonathan Harms complaint in Minnesota. In both of the California cases, OCR found against the schools and in favor of the complainants.

In the California cases, elementary school children were also involved, this time with boys as the alleged harassers and girls as the targets. The *Modesto* case began in January 1993, when several girls were restrained in choke holds, pinched, tripped, and touched repeatedly on their chests, genitalia, and buttocks by some male classmates. The school officials treated the incidences as routine misbehavior and followed their standard disciplinary procedures without determining if a sexually hostile environment existed. Nor were the parents informed of their rights under federal law Title IX. In May 1993, a group of boys, some of whom had been involved in the earlier incidences, threw two girls to the ground, forcibly kissed and fondled them, made lewd statements, and attempted to remove their clothing (Brown, 1994b). OCR's finding, issued on December 6, 1993, found that the school district had violated Title IX when it treated sexual harassment by elementary school students as a matter of misconduct and mischief rather than as a violation of federal antidiscrimination law.

The Newark (CA) case involved activity classically viewed and typically dismissed as mutual, voluntary, and playground behavior. "Friday flip-up" days were an institution at this school: on Fridays, the boys in the first through third grades flipped up the dresses of their female classmates. OCR found that this practice subjected the girls to teasing and touching based on their gender, created a different treatment for them, and limited their enjoyment of the educational program.

Gay Students

OCR issued a landmark ruling in the case of a gay student who had endured 2 years of abuse by other students. This voluntary settlement with the Fayetteville, Arkansas, school district was the first in which gay students were provided with coverage by federal law Title IX (*Fayetteville Public Schools, AR*, 1998).

This precedent-setting case involved a young man who was harassed and taunted throughout 1995 and 1996, and finally beaten by other students, suffering a broken nose and damage to his kidneys. The two students responsible for the beating were convicted of battery (Walsh, 1998a).

The agreement signed by the school district requires workshops for teachers and students, a commitment to take disciplinary action against any student "reported and confirmed to have engaged in sexually harassing behavior" (Walsh, 1998a, p. 30), and reports to OCR. The young man's lawyer, David S. Buckel, states: "School principals who question whether sexual harassment of gay students is illegal will learn a big lesson from this breakthrough" (Walsh, 1998a, p. 30).

CONCLUSIONS, IMPLICATIONS, AND LINGERING QUESTIONS FROM THE LAWSUITS AND COMPLAINTS

The California and Minnesota cases, which involve elementary school children, raise perplexing and disturbing questions: Are the ages of the targets and perpetrators the most salient factors that OCR considers when it decides to investigate a case? Or is it the sex of the target(s) and perpetrator(s)? Are incidents that involve children of the same sex exempt from reprisals if the students are in elementary school? What difference could the sex of the harassers or the target make when a student's clothes are pulled off? Are these acts not assault, let alone sexual harassment? Or is it that gendered violence doesn't register with some federal and school officials as real violence? (Stein, 1995a, p. 158).

Whether these questions are embedded in lawsuits in federal court or before investigators from the Office for Civil Rights, the answers given thus far have been different, varying by region of the country. The unintended consequence may be that at times it feels like we are living in different countries, defined by which federal district court or regional office of OCR has jurisdiction over a particular school district.

However, this journey has shown us that the courts are not clear or unified on the subject of sexual harassment in schools; at best, they may be reluctant participants. Judges, courtrooms, and legal decisions may not make the best teachers, even if they could give us clear, consistent, and unified guidance.

For educators, the following lessons can be drawn from lawsuits and complaints:

1. Regard the events from the student's perspective.
2. Consider the impact of even one event upon the overall climate of the school.

3. Think about the broader message that the reaction or lack of reaction conveys to the students.
4. Regard a student's complaint as worthy of investigation.

Yet, for purposes of this review, this journey through lawsuits and complaints has provided additional evidence that sexual harassment does indeed exist in our nation's schools, and that social scientists and educators ought to consider material, albeit messy and contradictory, that is available from lawsuits and complaints as more evidence attesting to the epidemic of the phenomenon of sexual harassment in our schools.

Bullying as Sexual Harassment in Elementary Schools

No DOUBT many of us can still conjure up the image of Jonathan Prevette, that cute little blond 6-year-old boy with thick glasses from Lexington, North Carolina, who said he kissed, at her request, a little 6-year-old girl classmate and was then accused of sexual harassment by his school district in late September 1996. While he, his parents, and the spokesperson for the school district could be found for several weeks on the evening news and talk shows, nothing was ever heard from the little girl and her parents. However, through a secondary source (Craig Koontz, chair of the school board), two journalists (Goodman, 1996; D. Nathan, personal communication, 1996) reported that the kiss was not mutual, that the little girl had not asked for it, that it was she who revealed the kiss to the school's administrators, and that she had subsequently blamed herself for all the fuss. However, as long as the parents of the little girl maintain their silence, the public will never know, and the little boy's version of the events will dominate.

According to the sociologist Laura O'Toole (1997), who did an analysis of 25 articles appearing in the national and regional press during a 2-week period at that time, one of the major motifs of the events as constructed by Jonathan's parents was that of Alfalfa, of *Little Rascals* fame. That metaphor may well indeed linger in the public's consciousness about this event, subsuming all rational discussion and analysis of the events, the context, and the actors.

A critical question that lies at the heart of this and any discussion of sexual harassment is that of mutuality. Had the kiss been mutually desired, requested, or performed, whether the children were 6 or 16, kissing might have been against school rules but it would not be sexual harassment—that is, behavior that is unwanted and unwelcomed. Yet, the fact that the school chose to cast this event as sexual harassment is revealing. On the one hand, it demonstrates their vigilance in regard to the existence of inappropriate, unwanted, and unwelcome behaviors of a sexual nature in schools. By leaping to call it sexual harassment, maybe they hoped to ward off litigation by the girl's family; fear of lawsuits with their negative publicity and monetary damage awards are a major concern for many school administrators and school board attorneys. On the other hand, the administrators' panic attack followed by their retraction that "we never called it sexual harassment," and the feeding frenzy of the press did nothing to illuminate the larger problem of bullying in schools or to acknowledge that sexual harassment could and does exist in elementary schools.

The interviews with the boy's family and with school officials reinforced for me the absurdity of attempting to have conversations with young children about sexual harassment. Common sense should lead us to use language and concepts that are already in young children's vocabulary to talk about interactions with their peers that are unwanted and wanted, whether those interactions are verbal, touching, or playing. I have found that the word and concept of *bullying* is one that young children understand and use, and may capture the coercive, invasive, unwanted, and intrusive nature of both bullying and sexual harassment. Unfortunately, never once did the national press during the Jonathan Prevette episode touch on this larger problem of bullying that is indeed omnipresent in children's lives.

In this chapter I will explore some of the research that has been conducted on bullying in schools, particularly bullying research that has a bearing on gender. However, in no way will this chapter be an exhaustive review of bullying research. I will discuss my preference, for educational and developmental reasons, for framing the problem of sexual harassment as bullying when we talk about it with children under the age of 10- or 11-years-old. Yet, by using the word bullying, I do not deny the existence of sexual harassment in elementary schools nor mean to imply that elementary schools are exempt from legal scrutiny (see Chapter 2); sexual harassment is against the law whereas bullying is not. Rather, I am voicing my opinion, confirmed somewhat by research, that with elementary-aged children, discussions framed as bullying rather than sexual harassment might be more developmentally appropriate.

BULLYING: DEFINITIONS AND RESEARCH

The antecedents of peer-to-peer sexual harassment in schools may be found in "bullying," behaviors children learn, practice, or experience beginning at a very young age. All boys know what a bully is, and many boys as well as girls have been victims of bullying. Much of the bullying that takes place at this age is between members of the same sex. Teachers and parents know about bullying, and many accept it as an unfortunate stage that some children go through on their way to adolescence and adulthood. Left unchecked and unchallenged, bullying may in fact serve as fertile practice ground for sexual harassment (Stein, 1993; 1995a).

Like its older cousin, sexual harassment, bullying deprives children of their rightful entitlement to be educated and secure in the knowledge that they will be safe and free from harm. Although laws in 38 states prohibit the practice of "hazing" in educational institutions (with hazing defined as the organized practice of induction, usually into a fraternity or sports team, through degrading behaviors, physical assault, or both), bullying floats free from legal restraint and adult intervention and is often not discussed as a deliberate part of the school curriculum (Stein, 1995a).

Scandinavia

The preeminent researcher in the world in the field of childhood-bullying research is Dan Olweus (1993, 1994), professor of psychology at the University of Bergen, Norway, who has conducted more than 20 years of research on bullying. His research has largely focused on Scandinavia: a study of 17,000 schoolchildren in Grades 3-9 in three cities in Sweden conducted in 1991; a study of 130,000 children in Norway, ages 8-16, representing almost a fourth of the whole student population in his country (1993); and a more detailed study, known as the Bergen (Norway) study of 2,500 boys and girls in Grades 4-7, along with data from 300 to 400 teachers and principals and 1,000 parents, on effects of an intervention program that he designed.

Before we try to import the findings from Olweus's research to children and schools in the United States, there are two major differences that need to be articulated. First of all, Sweden and Norway are largely homogenous countries, without much diversity in race, ethnicity, language, or religion—factors that often serve as triggers for bullying. Second, those countries, similar to most countries in Europe and the Western world, have a standardized, nationalized curriculum, allowing for more comparisons to be made across the country and classroom. Olweus's research and suggestions for interventions are predicated upon national regulation of the whole school environment, including classroom content, pedagogy, informal and formal activities, guidance and counseling, and activities to stimulate parental involvement.

Olweus defines bullying as activity occurring when someone is "exposed, repeatedly and over time, to negative actions on the part of one or more other students" (Olweus, 1993, p. 9; 1994). "Negative actions" for Olweus are intentional infliction or attempts at such, including threatening, taunting, teasing, name-calling, hitting, pushing, kicking, pinching, and restraining. He also acknowledges that it is possible to carry out negative actions "without the use of words or physical contact, such as by making faces or dirty gestures, intentionally excluding someone from a group, or refusing to comply with another person's wishes" (1993, p. 9). Bullying implies an imbalance of strength and can include a single incident of a serious nature, yet not all acts of meanness, pestering, or picking on someone constitute bullying. Olweus emphasizes that the salient feature of his definition of bullying is that the negative actions are repeated and carried out over time. Almost to a word, Olweus's definitions of bullying seem interchangeable with definitions of sexual harassment in the United States.

Olweus's major findings on bullying have indicated:

- Fifteen percent of all children are involved in bully/victim problems at some point in elementary and junior high. He estimates that approximately 7% of children have been bullies and 9% have been victimized, 3% have been bullied "about once a week or more frequently," and somewhat less than 2% bullied others at that rate (1993, p. 14).
- Boys tend to engage in more direct physical bullying than girls, but the most common forms of bullying among boys were with words and gestures.
- Boys were more often victims and, in particular, perpetrators of direct bullying.
- Girls engaged in more indirect bullying such as slandering, spreading rumors, and manipulation of friendships.
- Boys carried out much of the bullying that girls were subjected to: 60% of the bullied girls in Grades 5 through 7 reported being bullied mainly by boys; an additional 15–20% said they were bullied by both sexes, whereas 80% of boys said that they were bullied chiefly by boys.
- In secondary/junior high school, more than four times as many boys as girls reported having bullied other students.
- Bullying peaks in elementary school, and then decreases; there is a steady decline as children get older, meaning there is less of it at high school; however, a considerable part of the bullying that exists is carried out by older students, particularly in the earlier elementary grades.
- Most bullying happens in school rather than on the way to or from school, especially in those places where students tend to be less closely supervised by adults (playground, lunchroom, hallways); those students who were bullied on their way to and from school tended to be bullied at school, too.

- Parents and teachers are relatively unaware of the extent and intensity of bullying that exists. Children tend to underreport it to their parents and teachers due to embarrassment and fear of retaliation if the adult were to become involved.

In addition, Olweus's research has disclosed important information about the victims and bullies. He pointed out that there is not one universal type of bully or victim, so therefore a variety of interventions need to be designed for different kinds of bullies and different kinds of victims. Moreover, he refined the types of bullying into direct and indirect bullying (Ross, 1996). Moreover, the victims have no aberrant trait for the most part, though bullies may focus on or look for such a characteristic. It is important to note that according to Olweus (1993), having an aberrant trait is not the root cause of the bullying. Bullies are popular and have friends, whereas a victim is often a loner; popularity is likely to decrease a boy's risk of being bullied, and popularity is very tied to physical strength. Interestingly, Olweus points out that for girls, it is not clear whether any factor serves a similar protection function against bullying.

Olweus's research also laid to rest some myths that bullying is a big-city problem or that the size of the school or class is a salient feature. His research as well as that of another researcher in Finland (Lagerspetz, 1982, p. 24, in Olweus, 1993) gave no support at all to these hypotheses. He states conclusively that size of the class or school appears to be of negligible importance for the relative frequency or level of bully/victim problems in the class or the school. What does matter and have major significance in terms of the extent of bullying is the responses and attitudes of the adults in the school community.

Other countries have conducted research into bullying, including Canada (Pepler, Craig, Zeigler, & Charach, 1993); Japan (K. Hirano, personal communication as cited in Whitney & Smith, 1993, p. 5, and Olweus, 1993, p. 14); the Netherlands (Junger, 1990); Finland (Lagerspetz, Bjorqkvist, Berts, & King, 1982); Spain (Garcia & Perez, 1989); Australia (Rigby, Slee, & Conolly, 1991); and the United Kingdom.

United Kingdom

In the United Kingdom, initially the research was focused on single-sex boarding schools (Keise, 1992; Tattum & Lane, 1988; Tattum, 1993), but since the late 1980s, the research has expanded to include coed schools and racial bullying (Ahmad & Smith, 1994; Whitney & Smith, 1993; Tattum & Lane, 1988; Tattum, 1993; Tattum & Tattum, 1997). A valuable contribution from the British researchers has been their acknowledging and documenting the more indirect bullying and exclusion that is more typical of the repertoire of girls when they bully. Ahmad and Smith (1994) found in their research studies that whereas boys engaged in both verbal and physical abuse, girls were mainly involved in verbal abuse. Moreover, girls seemed to be more involved in perpetrating indirect bullying, which includes name-calling, gossip, rumors, secret-telling, refusing to be friends, refusing to allow someone to play, shunning, and playing tricks on someone.

In particular, two British studies illuminate the gendered nature of bullying. Whitney and Smith (1993) in their 1990 study of 6,700 students, ranging in age from 8 to 16 years old, in 24 schools in Sheffield found that the sex difference for being bullied is slight, but that girls tended to be bullied less than boys. In addition, boys admitted to bullying other boys considerably more than girls. They found that most bullying was carried out mainly by one boy; next came bullying by several boys, then mixed-sex bullying, followed by bullying by several girls, and least of all bullying by one girl. They found this pattern to be consistent in both junior/middle schools and secondary schools. Moreover, their research confirmed previous findings on gender differences: girls are equally likely to be bullied (slightly less so in secondary schools), but are only about half as likely to be involved in bullying others; and boys are bullied almost entirely by other boys, whereas girls are bullied by both sexes. Furthermore, boys are more involved in physical forms of bullying whereas girls specialize in more verbal and indirect forms. In other words, boys bully both sexes, often in physical ways, but girls bully only other girls, often in indirect ways. It remains, however, that the most common form of bullying is "being called nasty names" (p. 22), and that the playground is the most common location for bullying.

Smith, along with researcher Yvette Ahmad, reviewed sex differences in bullying. They state unequivocally that "sex differences in all forms of aggression have been repeatedly found, and bullying is no exception" (Ahmad & Smith, 1994, p. 70). In their own study they modified Olweus's (1993) definitions and accordingly the questionnaires to include forms of indirect bullying, which were not explicit in Olweus's original definitions, in order to be able to capture those forms of bullying in which girls typically engage. They surveyed over 1,400 students in five schools (two middle and three secondary) with a mixture of racial groups. Their results confirmed that boys are more involved than girls in bullying others, whether one is looking at indirect or direct bullying. Boys in both middle school and secondary school are usually bullied by other boys and rarely by girls. For girls, however, the picture is different: At the middle school level, they are most likely bullied by boys, but at the secondary level, they are most likely to be bullied by other girls (Ahmad & Smith, 1994). Moreover, for girls and boys in middle school, the playground is the most common site for bullying, but by secondary school, the most common site for girls becomes the classroom, then the corridors, whereas for boys, the playground remains the most common location.

Their results were similar to Whitney and Smith's 1993 study. They found that bullying decreased with age; boys were more likely than girls to report being bullied by one or several boys whereas girls were more likely than boys to report being bullied by one or several girls, or by both boys and girls; it was unusual for boys to report being bullied by one or several girls. Furthermore, boys were more likely to be physically hit and threatened than were girls, whereas girls were more likely to experience verbal forms of bullying (being called nasty names) and indirect bullying (such as no one talking to them). These sex differences were found in both middle and secondary schools. By secondary school, physical bullying has largely decreased for girls, but there is an escalation of their involvement in indirect bullying, especially spreading rumors about someone else (Ahmad & Smith, 1994, p. 81). Ahmad and Smith conclude that there are both qualitative and quantitative research findings that confirm the existence of male and female forms of bullying, but they assert that this finding does not mean that these forms are exclusive to each sex.

Canada

Recent studies in Canada (1991-1995), summarized in a paper by O'Connell and colleagues (1997), include for the first time a study of 588 children in Grades 1-3, the first study of bullying and victimization problems among such young children.

Results from this younger sample included the following developmental differences: Peers intervened (at 24% of the incidents) in bullying episodes for Grades 1-3 as opposed to interventions in Grades 4-6 (at 11% of the time) or Grades 7-8 (at 7% of the time). Other developmental differences emerged when the students were asked, "Could you join in bullying?" In Grades 1-3, 12% of the children answered yes, whereas 31% in Grades 4-6 said yes, compared to 49% in Grades 7-8. The final striking developmental difference was in the realm of willingness to help the victim. In short, it declined with age: 57% of the students in Grades 1-3 were willing, but only 39% in Grades 4-6, and 27% in Grades 7-8. Indeed, the cumulative results of this study provide a sad portrait of aging, compassion, and empathy.

Moreover, these Canadian studies showed a decline in adult involvement in bullying episodes. Children in the younger grades (1-3) reported higher (37%) adult interventions as opposed to 26% in Grades 4-6, and only 30% in Grades 7 and 8. In summary, the Canadian researchers found that with age children were more willing to join in the bullying and less willing to help a victim, and that there was a decrease in reports of peers helping victims. This final finding is consistent with the finding of decreased concern for victims in Rigby et al.'s (1991) Australian study.

United States

In the United States, on the other hand, most of the initial research on bullying was designed from a psychological/psychopathological point of view. There seems to have been a tendency to pathologize the problem, with a focus on bullies or on treatment programs to rid them of their bullying tendencies or to develop guideposts by which to judge potential bullies. Largely this research has consisted of interviews with criminals, including jailed molesters or pedophiles who traced back their conduct and behavior. Although this methodology may illuminate their trajectories, it is not a particularly good measure for making generalizations about normative behavior for the majority of boys and men.

Several recent studies have focused on school-aged children in the United States. A study conducted by Oliver, Hazler, and Hoover (1994) looked at children in Grades 7–12, and found that girls, significantly more than boys, felt that bullies had higher social status than did their victims. This study also found that even in small-town, allegedly safe environments, 81% of the males and 72% of the females reported being bullied by their peers, with ridicule and verbal and social harassment as the most common forms.

A second study from the Center for Adolescent Studies at Indiana University of 558 middle-school boys and girls found that bullies, compared with other children, faced more forceful parental discipline at home, spent less time with adults, and had fewer positive adult role models or positive peer influences (Seppa, 1996). Gender was not teased out in this study.

The work of two U.S. researchers have a bearing on the issue of gender-based teasing and bullying. Barrie Thorne's book *Gender Play: Girls and Boys in School* (1993), although not explicitly about bullying, certainly raises questions about the nature of gendered play and interactions, and offers many insights into the development of gender relations in elementary school. She found that boys use sexual insults against girls, and that they regard girls as a group as a source of contamination. Boys and girls who don't conform to this prototype, and especially those who desire to be friends with one another, are at risk of teasing or ostracization. One girl, speaking of her friendship with a boy, at church and in their neighborhood, poignantly offers the reason why they don't speak to each other at school: "We pretend not to know each other so we won't get teased" (p. 50). The threat of heterosexual teasing may act as a deterrent to cross-gender friendships or may drive those friendships underground.

In addition, Donna Eder and colleagues at Indiana University in their book *School Talk: Gender and Adolescent Culture* (1995), and in a more recent book chapter (Eder, 1997), studies sexual aggression within the culture of middle school students. She and her colleagues have studied language and informal talk in middle school, including gossip, teasing, insulting, and story-telling. As with the European studies, Eder found that boys and girls alike used sexual put-downs toward girls, and that girls' use of words such as *sluts* or *whores* helped to maintain a hierarchy with male-oriented, tough, and sexu-ally aggressive boys at the top. Girls also tormented boys who were friendly toward them by casting doubt on their heterosexuality. Eder points out these and other ways in which girls contribute indirectly towards sexual aggression.

Finally, my own research into sexual harassment through the survey in the September 1992 issue of *Seventeen* magazine garnered responses from girls as young as 9 and 10 years old. Out of 4,300 surveys returned by the time of the deadline, we randomly selected 2,000 of them to be analyzed (Stein, Marshall, & Tropp, 1993); of those 2,000 surveys, one came from a 9-year-old; seven from 10-year- olds, 38 from 11-year-olds, and 226 from 12-year-olds. There was no doubt from their responses that girls even at this young age knew about gender-based harassment—either from their own experiences or from observing it happening in their schools (see Chapter 1).

PILOT STUDIES ON BULLYING

In the winter of 1993, I began a small pilot project that involved seven class-rooms in three elementary schools in Boston and Brookline, Massachusetts. For a period of 8–10 weeks, I developed and taught fourth- and fifth-grade students a variety of lessons on teasing and bullying. Over the course of the following 2 years, these classroom lessons were further refined by some of the teachers and me, and were finally published as a teaching guide on teas-ing and bullying (Sjostrom & Stein, 1996).

Beginning in October 1995, further research was funded by the U.S. Department of Education (Women's Educational Equity Act Project, and Safe and Drug-Free Schools and Communities Act) to look at gender-based teasing and bullying in Grades K–3. With research partners in New York City (Educa-tional Equity Concepts), our research was conducted at one elementary school on the Upper West Side of New York City that had a student population of mixed ethnic and socioeconomic status as well as in three schools in Framing-ham, Massachusetts. The three Framingham schools have a student popula-tion that is predominately White but with a sizable number of ethnic minor-ity students, including Hispanic, African American, and Asian, and recent immigrants from the Azores and Eastern Europe. In addition, at two out of the three Massachusetts schools, there were students who lived in homeless shelters or shelters for battered women. The faculty in all the schools, in both cities, were almost exclusively White women, a major limitation of our research that will restrict the generalizations that can be drawn from this project.

In both cities, the schools that participated were self-selected; the principals were more or less recruited, as were the classroom teachers. In Massachusetts, we observed more than 450 children in a total of 17 classrooms in Grades K–3, as well as conducted interviews with 27 individual children. The children whom we interviewed were selected by the teachers to provide a sampling of those identified by teachers as initiators, recipients, or bystanders of bullying. Within each grade level, there were equal numbers of girls and boys interviewed. The sample of 27 students included numbers of children who were of different racial and socioeconomic backgrounds: one half of them were White, and the other half were Asian, African American, Hispanic, or biracial; four were children with an identifiable special need.

Moreover, we conducted focus groups with teachers and a separate set for parents at each of the schools. A total of 24 teachers participated in our focus groups, including teachers from Grades K–5, plus bilingual, special education, art, physical education, and music teachers. About 50 parents attended the information meetings that were held at two schools, but only 10 of the parents were able to actually participate in the organized focus group.

Within the parameters of our research, our results mirrored those of Olweus's as outlined above. We found that the responses and attitudes of the adults had major significance on the extent of bullying that occurred. In fact, we could identify distinct trends in the three different schools, with the principal's leadership style and responses playing a central role that also had a bearing upon the teachers' responses to children's teasing and bullying. In addition, the tone and climate that the teachers set in the classroom had an impact on the incidence of teasing and bullying that we observed. Our observations at two of the schools with the greatest difficulties, and later confirmed by comments from the teacher focus groups, pointed toward a lack of respect by the teachers toward their students and their families. Teachers tended to use authoritarian measures, such as yelling at students, or making comments that embarrassed them or demeaned them.

Findings from the Children

The interviews with the children confirmed and corroborated both our observations and the information provided by the teachers in the focus groups. This notwithstanding, the parents and teachers doubted the veracity of what the children would reveal to us; the adults assumed that the children would invent events or distort reality. However, the students we interviewed told it like we saw it.

In the Massachusetts sites, we observed little overt gender-based teasing and bullying except for teasing about body parts, and incidents of exclusion by gender. However, teachers and parents reported gender-based incidents largely occurring on the buses or in bathrooms. According to the parents and teachers, these incidents involved same-sex initiators and recipients. On the other hand, we observed numerous incidents of class and racially based bullying; for example, students were singled out because they were Hispanic or poor, new immigrants were targeted, students were excluded from informal-time playing on the basis of their appearance or ethnicity or both. Interestingly, we observed several students with obvious disabilities, but they were not targeted for their disabilities (one wonders if teasing about disabilities was "off limits").

There were some incidents of gender-based exclusion or teasing that we couldn't adequately document because those events were not overt or we were unable to hear comments or talk among the children. These gender-based incidents included two salient interactions. The first revealing incident that was typical and repeatedly occurred at both indoor and outdoor play times, when groups of girls or boys were able to effectively exclude (or systematically eliminate) opposite-sex peers by setting rules or tasks that the opposite-sex peers either couldn't or wouldn't follow. Examples from such strategies were giving opposite-sex peers undesirable roles in a game (roles that were eliminated once the offending peer, usually a boy, left), or creating new rules such as hitting hard slams during ball games, which stopped once the peer (usually girls) left. At no point did we overhear gendered exclusion spoken about; in other words, we never heard "no boys allowed" or "girls can't play with us." Whatever code was operating was unspoken and subtle, yet it was fully operative.

The second salient event occurred during recess at one school, where the boys typically played with balls and the girls typically played with jump ropes. Often these items were brought from home because the school didn't have any to offer to the children (particularly jump ropes); without these items, there was virtually nothing for the children to do other than run around the playground. In previous weeks, the boys had been teasing the girls by making a game of stealing their ropes. The teachers had become so annoyed at the fussing that resulted (girls complaining to the teachers about the boys' behavior) that the teachers responded by prohibiting jump ropes from the playground, thereby effectively taking away the girls' play. The boys seemed to recognize this development as a gendered triumph.

Our interviews with children about their experiences in schools produced findings similar to those reported in other research studies (Ahmad & Smith, 1994; Olweus, 1993, 1994). Those results include:

- Transition time, lunch, and recess were times when teasing and bullying were most likely to occur.
- Teasing and bullying were most prevalent when adults were not present, not paying attention, or not physically available. In the Massachusetts schools where we observed, transition times, recess, lunch, arrival, and departure times were supervised by untrained parent volunteers or other low-paid employees, individuals whom the children viewed as people without much authority. Moreover, at these times, adult-to-child ratios were very high.
- When students go to adults, or when adults witness incidents of teasing and bullying, the students feel they are not listened to or taken seriously; they are often admonished to work it out on their own. Ironically, the students felt that they were doing just what the adults told them to do, which was to try to work out their problems with other students, and if that didn't work, then they should tell an adult. But when they did approach an adult, students got a conflicting message because the adults were typically annoyed and impatient and seemed to brush them off by telling the child to go back and deal with it on his or her own. The adults typically didn't give students helpful guidance about how to do this, nor did they give support to them for attempting to do it.
- Students felt that perpetrators were not punished; many children felt that the consequences (such as going to the principal's office) were fun, and did not carry a negative connotation or consequence. The victims were then often subjected to more teasing either because they told (other words for this behavior include *ratted*, *dimed*, *squealed*) or because the teasers felt that they could get away with it, because the adult hadn't intervened. So the cycle continued and often escalated.
- Students surmised that children resort to bullying for fun or because they're bored.

As one might expect, when the adults were asked about this cycle, they put an entirely different spin on the events. Both parents and teachers felt that students came to them with very trivial concerns, and couldn't understand why the children couldn't work out these problems on their own. Nonetheless, teachers also frequently complained that principals trivialized their concerns with teasing and bullying, claiming that they had more important or difficult issues to manage, usually problems that involved the older students in the school. Teachers complained and hypothesized that if the little problems in Grades K–3 were appropriately handled with discipline, then there wouldn't be as many big issues in the upper grades.

From our observations and interviews with the children, it seemed that first the students were asking for better and more effective skills (what to say;

models of conduct) to manage their problems on their own, and second for support, authority, and a belief in their attempts to deal with the offending peer. What we found particularly disturbing about this cycle was that it echoed exactly what my research has found with older students about their experiences of sexual harassment—that it happens in public, that adults were often watching, and that when students reported the sexual harassment to the adults, the adults either did not believe the students, trivialized the problem, or dismissed the events entirely.

Results from Focus Groups with Parents and Teachers

Two sets of separate focus groups were held, one set with parents and a separate set with teachers. The results revealed that both parents and teachers felt that teasing and bullying were problems that existed both at school and at home with siblings, and that the problem seemed to be getting worse, in both the amount and degree of teasing and bullying. The following is a long list of the behaviors that the adults noticed about teasing and bullying behaviors in children:

- "Teases du jour": cooties; being fat (directed at girls more than boys)
- Talk about "dating" or "love" (even among second and third graders); threatening to kiss or hug another child, a threat particularly used by girls toward boys
- "Meanness" which usually meant exclusion, won't be friends, name-calling; focusing on a feature of a child's appearance, typically their clothing, which seemed to be a stand-in for a socioeconomic-class commentary
- Put-downs that involved one's mother ("your mother . . .")
- Physical behaviors that usually involved boys on boys; giving another child a wedgies (that is, picking up a child by their underwear), pantsing (which means pulling down a child's pants, or underwear)
- Body-part talk (especially boys teasing other boys about the size or shape of their penis)
- Using the F-word ("f———you") toward other adults as well as other kids
- Taking the possessions of other children
- Telling a child that he or she is a member of the opposite sex: "you kick/ throw/[etc.] like a girl" and "you look like a boy/girl"
- Using derogatory words about sexual preference (*gay, fag, lezzie*) or race or ethnic background (*nigger, spic*)
- Proclaiming "I don't like so-and-so because s/he's a ——— [racial epithet]"; calling girls "bitches"

Both parents and teachers indicated that they thought the children really did not understand the meaning of the words that they used, but knew that the words were bad. They also noted that verbal teasing quickly escalated to physical acts between students. In particular, teachers focused on

- Absence of students' qualms about swearing at or threatening teachers (e.g., "You can't touch me!")
- Lack of support from principals (e.g., being sent to the principal's office was considered fun for students, and principals were afraid to take a stand against teasing and bullying)
- Lack of support from administrators (ineffectiveness of guidance counselors designated to deal with serious or longstanding behavioral difficulties)
- Principals not taking a stand with teachers who exhibited disrespectful or bullying behaviors
- Principals being more concerned with older students and trivializing difficulties with the younger students
- Too much leeway being given to children from so-called troubled backgrounds (e.g., "Don't do it again, OK?")
- Lack of consistent, effective policies that held consequences for teasing and bullying (something beyond detentions, or telling the offending students, even those in kindergarten, to "write until their hands fall off" as a punishment for most infractions)
- Frequency of stealing, fighting, and problems on the bus

IS BULLYING SEXUAL HARASSMENT?

The simple answer is yes, but if it is a boy-to-girl interaction, then it is more likely to be labeled as sexual harassment than if the interactions occurred between same-sex members or if it involved behaviors that came from girls directed toward boys; rarely are same-sex behaviors deemed to be sexual harassment. However, if all the protagonists are in elementary school, then sexual harassment will rarely be acknowledged. Words such as *pestering, annoying, bothering, hassling,* or *bugging* will more than likely creep into descriptions of the events; the law will rarely be seen as operative or having application. Yet, since sexual harassment is against the law, and bullying is not, more students, their families, and lawyers will try to frame the events as sexual harassment, rather than as bullying, regardless of the ways that school administrators try to characterize the incidents. Irrespective of the ways in which school officials frame or dismiss the incidents, parents may file self-standing criminal complaints against the individuals involved, as opposed to being limited to filing civil court actions against the school district and personnel. As I discussed at length in Chapter 2, there have been lawsuits and complaints that involved children in elementary schools (fifth grader Aurelia

Davis in federal court in Georgia; third grader Jonathan Harms and first grader Cheltzie Hentz in Minnesota under Minnesota state law; and the U.S. Department of Education's Office for Civil Rights complaints in Modesto and Newark, California, that both involved elementary school students).[1]

Although much of Olweus's research findings about children's behaviors might qualify as sexual harassment under U.S. law (Title IX), with liability falling on the school system, he never discusses sexual harassment. Nonetheless, his definition of bullying has many parallels to sexual harassment, particularly in the repeated and long-term nature of the behaviors targeted against an individual. Severity is not the salient feature in his definition of bullying; similarly with sexual harassment, severity is not the ruling feature: *repeated* and *pervasive* are defining terms that carry as much weight.

Our research in Grades K-3 points toward the existence of conduct that could be labeled and possibly litigated as sexual harassment. Our research also indicates the usefulness of conducting classroom discussions and a whole-school approach toward bullying; it is developmentally appropriate and seems to engage the students, appearing both relevant and helpful.

If educators and advocates pose and present the problem as "bullying" to young children, rather than labeling it immediately as "sexual harassment," we can engage children and universalize the phenomenon as one that boys as well as girls will understand and accept as problematic. Hopefully, such an approach will go a long way toward engendering compassion and empathy in the students. Moreover, we can simultaneously avoid demonizing all little boys as potential "harassers" by initially presenting these hurtful and offensive behaviors as bullying, a behavior found in the repertoire of both boys and girls. Activities that ask the children to distinguish between "teasing" and "bullying" can help them focus on the boundaries between appropriate and inappropriate, hurtful behaviors.

Returning to the voices of children, the reflections of fifth graders at the end of the 8-10 week unit on teasing and bullying display new conceptual connections as well as insights about themselves and their classmates.

> Well, since we started this, people in my class and I learned a lot. Now they stopped doing mean things to each other. Like now that people know how I felt when they called me "shrimp" and "shorty" and other mean things they stopped doing that. Now we don't hurt other people's feelings and respect one another even if the person is short, tall or opposite sex. (male)

> I see a big difference in myself since we started discussing bullying, teasing and sexual harassment. Example: when it was my turn to be captain of the kickball game I picked x as a player. As soon as I picked x, he started to pick all the players and suddenly x was the captain. Not only that but x also picked who was pitcher and the batting order (all stuff captain does). So, I stood up to x

reminded him that I was captain (I would have never done that before). It made me feel good inside. (female)

I do see a difference in the way that all of the boys in the class are treating the girls now. 1) they have mostly stopped teasing us and chasing us down the hallways while we are coming back from recess. 2) The boys have also mostly stopped insulting all of the girls and trying to dis us. I think that the girls have also mostly stopped teasing and bullying all of the shrimpy or short boys. (female)

I really think sexual harassment can hurt because sometimes people may tease you about your body parts and it really hurts your feelings because you can't change them in any way. It can also interfere with your school work because all your thoughts are on your anger and then you can't concentrate. If I am harassed in the future, I will stand up for my rights and if a teacher doesn't care, I will pressure him or her to punish my harasser. (male) (Stein, 1995a, p. 150)

Gaining a conceptual framework and common vocabulary that elementary-school-age children can understand, apply, and reapply will help them find their own links between teasing and bullying and sexual harassment. The connection between bullying and sexual harassment in schools is of critical importance—it is one that educators need to make explicit and public by deliberately discussing these subjects in age-appropriate ways with children.

4

Misapplication of Sexual Harassment

HAVING TRAVELED through many lawsuits and complaints as well as less litigious ways of framing the problem of sexual harassment among younger children as bullying, we have a clearer sense of the common and prototypical features of sexual harassment in schools, at least those that get a hearing in the courts or in state and federal agencies that investigate sexual harassment allegations. Beyond our merely noticing the varying opinions and decisions that the courts are rendering in peer-to-peer sexual harassment cases, we may characterize the courts as reluctant participants in the negotiation of the territory of appropriate behavior. In fact, using the courts, even in the best cases, may not provide much clarity or guidance for school personnel elsewhere in the country. They should be the route of last resort for the resolution of the problem.

We now turn to the schools and all of their players to examine how sexual harassment and its larger parent, sex discrimination, have been understood. To the layperson, the term *sexual harassment* conjures up both legal and colloquial meanings. In this chapter, we will be looking at conceptual confusions that exist on the ground between what students think of as sex discrimination and their ideas about sexual harassment; and at attempts to regulate student expression, especially when it is characterized as sexual harassment.

First, we need a summary of the federal law that outlaws sex discrimination. Title IX of the Education Amendments of 1972 was passed by Congress to outlaw sex discrimination in education. Before Title IX, there were very limited athletic opportunities for girls and women, sometimes consisting only of cheerleading squads or one sports team per season (field hockey in the fall, basketball in winter, and softball in the spring). In elementary schools, girls were prevented from serving on safety patrol; in high school, girls took home economics and boys took shop—those borders could not be crossed; and women teachers in K-12 schools had to leave their jobs when they became pregnant, and students who became pregnant were forced to accept home tutoring or sent to a school-in-exile so they wouldn't be seen by other students. To say that our schools were not bastions of democracy is an understatement.

With the passage of Title IX in 1972, a multitude of provisions were created to end sex discrimination in education. Parity in athletic opportunities and funding for females is probably the aspect of federal law Title IX that has received the most attention and dissension. Other provisions of the law include the educational rights of pregnant and parenting students, admission to schools receiving federal financial assistance regardless of sex, equal access to courses and activities regardless of sex, employment opportunities regardless of sex, and the establishment of grievance procedures. In addition, through legal precedent established by lawsuits, Title IX has come to cover sexual harassment in education, though the words *sexual harassment* appear nowhere in the original law.

As the term *sexual harassment* has traveled into the schoolhouse, it has come to be misapplied or overapplied in some cases, whereas in other cases has acted as the threat that has saved a student or group of students from persistent torment and harassment. The major irony and paradox seems to be that as students have misapplied and overapplied the term, either because they literally do not know the expression *sex discrimination*, or because they have learned about the limitations of that term as opposed to the power of *sexual harassment*, they have inadvertently played right into the tendencies of school administrators to curb students' rights of free expression (First Amendment rights).

Students are always testing the limits of their First Amendment rights, whether in the realm of student publications, assemblies, dress, or spoken words. They would never knowingly participate in the reduction of those rights; their raison d'être is to push the envelope. School officials, on the other hand, live to put limitations on student expression, and are often engaged in conflicts with students about their rights of speech, dress, publication, and assembly. Usually, school administrators win those battles, be they in the courtroom or in the schoolhouse, and are rarely intimidated or threatened when students assert their First Amendment rights.

However, with the advent of sexual harassment litigation, and the term *sexual harassment* being bandied about more frequently by students and adults alike, school officials have become very jumpy and often crack down on students' words and actions, using the context of sexual harassment as their justification. To the extent that students are participating in this frenzy and overapplication and misapplication, they are in essence contributing to the reduction of their First Amendment rights, silencing their own voices and restricting their own activities.

It is now our task to probe the ways in which the label of sexual harassment is misapplied or overapplied, whether by school officials or students, and to understand the ways in which this might reduce the First Amendment rights of students.

ATMOSPHERE OF PANIC AND CONFUSION

The fear of lawsuits, both against the school district and against individual employees, coupled with a longstanding propensity to attempt to regulate and censor student behaviors, has caused a lot of panicked school personnel and state officials to initiate and support the passing of state laws and educational regulations about sexual harassment in education.

California is a case in point. The laws on sexual harassment in education that California passed on January 1, 1993, are ones that embody panic posing as progressive tendencies. The laws require that (1) each school must develop a policy on sexual harassment and post it in the school, (2) the policy must be mailed home, and (3) students may be suspended and expelled if they have "committed" sexual harassment (California Education Code, sections 48900.2, 212.5, 212.6).

My concerns flow from each of these California laws. First of all, it is foolish bordering on humorous to assume that posting a piece of paper compels people, especially if they are young, to read it. Since the law doesn't require that the policy be read aloud, it is rather ludicrous to assume that most students would read something posted by adults, especially if the notice is written in legalese. Second, there is no requirement to translate the sexual harassment policy into any language other than English. If estimates are accurate that approximately 50% of the children of California do not speak English as their first language, mailing copies of the new sexual harassment laws to their homes in English may be a very futile and expensive gesture. Finally, there is no requirement to conduct preventive training or discussions with the students prior to suspending or expelling them. The preventive education provisions of this bill were removed before it became law largely because of the anticipated expenses that either the state or the school districts would have had to undertake. Thus, there is no requirement to offer education for the whole student body; education is offered only in the service of discipline once a student has been designated as a potential harasser.

Very few groups lined up against this law, but among them were the California chapter of the American Civil Liberties Union, the Mexican American Legal Defense and Education Fund (MALDEF), and the San Francisco-based feminist legal organization Equal Rights Advocates. Any time I was interviewed by the California or national press (Orenstein, 1994; Wagner & Coats, 1992) around the time of the law's passage in January 1993, I spoke out against this law—for its very punitive measures, which I feared that would push students out of school faster than they were already leaving. However, some feminist groups in California such as the American Association of University Women consider this law to be a victory, or at least a start.

Concurrent with the development of punitive state laws has been the rise of a small growth industry—companies that offer videos and curricula to buy, and training consultants to hire, with the purpose of immunizing the purchaser's school district. Among much useful material, however, reside pockets of bad advice and simplistic pedagogy and the invention of legal theory by some of these self-anointed experts. How is a well-meaning, let alone panicked, school official to distinguish the useful from the bogus, and potentially dangerous, cavalier advice?

The panic is also generated by the students themselves, who may be misapplying the label *sexual harassment* to incidents that would best be described as sex discrimination. Students and adults alike are familiar with the term *sexual harassment* and not necessarily *sex discrimination*—that expression isn't exactly in the common parlance of most students (except those who are aware of athletic budgets that are disproportionately divided between the boys' teams and girls' teams). Students also know that they can get attention and bring everything to a screeching halt by labeling particular incidents and behaviors as sexual harassment. In some ways the students are reading the culture accurately—since when, in the 20 years of Title IX prior to the *Franklin* decision in 1992, did anything come to a screeching halt if you called it sex discrimination? Not often.

One perfect example of the misapplication of the term *sexual harassment* occurs when teenage boys declare to their female counterparts: "Your skirt (shorts, shirt, dress, hair, makeup, etc.) is sexually harassing me." Armed with this 1990s lingo, teenage boys across America have redefined sexual harassment, casting themselves as victims of girls' clothes, makeup, hair, looks, and the like. Boys flaunt their new victimhood status to their female counterparts and also assert their claim to teachers and administrators who are enforcing, be it from enlightenment or jitters, new codes of conduct that have been created to prevent and eliminate sexual harassment. However, not far beneath the surface of this clever, even humorous, statement lie feelings of confusion, resentment, and in some cases hostility, directed at both the girls and at the adults in the school community.

On one hand, these words, "your skirt is sexually harassing me," are a measure of our success. The expression *sexual harassment* has been absorbed into the vocabulary of adolescents in the past several years, and in some instances the term is used accurately (Stein, 1995b). In addition, some boys have learned the lesson that commonplace behaviors, gestures, and expressions that were formerly part of their daily repertoire are now considered suspect, if not legally defined as sexual harassment. Thus, they have toned down or eliminated, at least in public in front of their teachers, some of the overtly assaultive behaviors such as bra-snapping, tittie-twisting, skirt-flipping, pants-pulling-down, and body groping.

However, in the place of crude remarks and behaviors, other boys have instituted a new version of the old tune of blaming the victims/targets—that is, trying to hold girls responsible for boys' responses and reactions. What used to be phrased as "your skirt is turning me on," and therefore "I'm out of control; I am not responsible for my conduct," has been transformed into "Your skirt is sexually harassing me." And, with this new reconceptualization, boys then claim that the girls have violated the school's sexual harassment policy.

The confusion and resentment can be traced to a variety of sources. Conduct that was once permitted, overlooked, or regarded as typical adolescent behaviors or constructed as "flirting" and normative has been labeled in the past few years as sexual harassment (Easton, 1994; Eaton, 1993; Pitsch, 1994b; Stein, 1992a, 1992b, 1993a, 1993b, 1995b). This reformulation comes as a great shock to many boys, who asserted when chastised, "No one ever told me that I couldn't do that." Indeed, there is truth in that statement, and the gap in their knowledge may well lie at the feet of school personnel who rarely named or interrupted inappropriate gendered harassment.

It is also the case that many boys are loath to give up what they regarded as their entitlement to pat, pinch, touch, and grope girls. In a very short period of time, boys perceive that the girls have been presented with a new power over them—that of labeling certain behaviors as sexual harassment. Once girls claim the (legal) power to designate particular conduct as sexual harassment, boys are at the mercy of the school's sexual harassment policy and procedures, accompanied, to the boys' ways of thinking, by unwarranted hassles and reprisals. Boys find themselves getting into trouble, sometimes big trouble, ranging from reprimands, suspensions, expulsions, criminal complaints, and lawsuits for conduct now called sexual harassment. Time now to address the question of false accusations.

FALSE ACCUSATIONS OR MISAPPLICATION OF TERMS?

There have been no studies that have looked at the issue of false complaints in K–12 schools. Nonetheless, the specter of false complaints remains and may serve to undermine efforts to implement sexual harassment policies and procedures and to minimize the reports that students bring to the attention of the school officials.

The problem or folklore of false accusations among peers is everyone's greatest fear, and often among the first statements uttered when a complaint has been filed against a particular student(s). The standard line of thinking often goes something like this: She filed a complaint because she wanted to get back at him; she was jealous, wanted attention, has an ax to grind ever since _____ (fill in the blank). I believe that it is possible to consider the accused person/student(s) as innocent until proven guilty without deeming the complaint to be false or fabricated.

The only way to answer this nagging and volatile question is to extrapolate from higher education (a method that may have little or no bearing on the K–12 context). False complaints are widely feared, but remain very rare even in the higher education context. In a study of 311 campus sexual harassment policies and procedures conducted by the Indiana University Office of Women's Affairs in 1984 (this is the most recent study on the subject of false complaints that was available), false complaints were found to be about 5% of all complaints filed (Robertson, Dyer, & Campbell, 1988). The study noted that this figure was probably a conservative estimate because university officials had no incentive to minimize the issue of false claims.

Survey respondents were asked, "How many complaints, if any, have you received which were proven to be intentionally fabricated?"and 82% of the respondents said none. The authors wrote:

> In all, 64 false complaints were reported from the other 18% of the schools (n = 46), 12% report(ed) one only and 6% two to four. For purposes of comparison, there were 425 documented and 760 estimated complaints received in 1982–83. (p. 800)

Indeed, the term *false* is used very loosely and has different meanings to different people. A complaint is not "false" as in *fabricated* if it was dismissed for lack of sufficient evidence to make a determination, or because everyone involved couldn't agree on what had happened or if the sexual harassment had not reached a standard to trigger an investigation. Moreover, complaints are sometimes dismissed for technical (such as the amount of time that has elapsed since the last incident) rather than substantive grounds, which would not mean that there wasn't harassment or injury.

Unfortunately, as there are no comparable studies of false complaints in the K–12 arena, we are left with only folklore about students who have been falsely accused, who endured shame and punishment only later, when the story was retracted, to be redeemed. We clearly need research into this area so we can obtain an accurate picture.

I have another theory about the phenomenon of false complaints in K–12 schools. Whether directing the charge of sexual harassment against their peers or against teachers, students are well aware that they can garner attention and get everything to come to a screeching halt if they label an incident as sexual harassment. Students may be misapplying this label to incidents that would best be described as sex discrimination.

CENSORSHIP: THE LARGER CONTEXT OF SCHOOLING

Sexual harassment that occurs in schools needs to be seen within the context of the whole school environment. Thus, we need to recall that schools are extremely hierarchical environments, which are regulated by law, by judicial precedent, by administrative practice, and by authoritarian whim. For the students, schools are the closest thing to the government, and their presence there is compulsory. Herein lies the tension and paradox of sexual harassment within a context where student expression is regulated, contested, and broached.

In 1969, through the U.S. Supreme Court case *Tinker v. Des Moines School District*, in an antiwar protest consisting of their wearing black armbands, high school students from Iowa helped to establish that public school students do not shed their constitutional rights to freedom of speech or expression at the schoolhouse gate. However, the past two decades have seen a continued erosion of First Amendment privileges (speech and press) and abrogations of Fourth Amendment guarantees against illegal searches (freedom of speech in *Bethel School District v. Fraser*, 1986; freedom of the press in *Hazelwood School District v. Kuhlmeier*, 1988; and searches and seizures in *New Jersey v. T.L.O.*, 1985).

It is common practice in many schools for students to pass through metal detectors upon entering the school and to wear or carry picture identification cards; for lockers, backpacks, and purses to be searched; and for library books, plays, school newspapers, and classroom reading lists to be censored. There is often a dress code that excludes earrings for boys; halter tops, shorts, and miniskirts for girls; and tight jeans, baggy jeans, certain colors, hats, and T-shirts with rock groups or political slogans for anyone. In fact, in some schools, not even the First Amendment printed out on a T-shirt would be allowed; nor a T-shirt with the peace symbol—it was construed to be a sign of "Devil worship" in Pasadena, Texas. A 12-year-old student in one of the six schools in Pasadena that banned the peace symbol noted, "If they ban peace symbols, they'll have to ban basic geometry because of all its lines and circles" (People for the American Way, 1990, pp. 79–80).

Given this pattern of censorship in schools, one might think that sexually harassing speech would be stamped out without any regard to the First Amendment. But, no, lots of sexist and harassing behaviors escape notice and condemnation from school authorities. There are countless examples of laxity of adult scrutiny. Consider the circulation of multiple copies of lists that demean and vulgarize girls; this is what the advent of home computers have enabled students to do. Examples have included "slam books," collections of writings, sexual "testimonials," and dirty drawings submitted by groups of boys at Santa Clara High School, California, about particular girls (see Chapter 2); "magna cum slutty" lists distributed in everyone's locked mail box at an elite boarding school in the East[1]; "piece of ass of the week" list at a private day school[2]; and the "25 most fuckable girls" list at a public school in Chaska, Minnesota (*Olson v. Independent School District #112*, 1991), which the *New York Times* called "the 25 most promiscuous" (Gross, 1992; to say that something is lost in the translation is an understatement).

NO FIRST AMENDMENT RIGHT TO SEXUALLY HARASS

Students, with or without adult approval and consent, often invoke the First Amendment as a justification for sexist, even sexually harassing, conduct. A typical example recounted by a middle school teacher in Massachusetts (personal communication, April 1994) involved a case where a student circulated a piece of paper, asking the other students to vote on whether they thought a particular boy was a "girl" or a "boy." When the teacher interceded and confiscated the paper, the originator of this tally claimed that their First Amendment rights were being violated by the teacher. "No," said the teacher, "you are disrupting the class, and that takes precedence."

The First Amendment is also used as justification to maintain the ever popular "kickline." Usually part of a school pep rally, to engender school spirit, one of the male sports teams dresses up in drag, dons wigs and skirts, inserts balloons or nerf balls into their shirts, and writes the names or nicknames of various cheerleaders on their individual T-shirts. This school-sponsored activity is sometimes held in the high school during the school day, with required attendance, or after school, open to the whole community; in other towns the kickline is also performed during the half-time show at sporting events. Imagine, if you will, that this kickline mocked kids with physical disabilities or a kickline where students dressed in Ku Klux Klan outfits. My hunch is that such kicklines would not be allowed to perform, repeatedly. Most likely, the performers would be yanked off the stage, having offended adult sensibilities. But, when the subject of the mockery is girls, it is an activity that is seen as being in the national interest, or at least as a healthy contribution to adolescent development.

This kickline ritual can be found in schools across the nation, from Maine to Montana to Alaska to Texas and everywhere in between. Teachers are often the first to acknowledge that such a kickline has been performed in their school building. Some of those very same teachers have publicly suggested alternatives to offensive "outfits"—just do the kickline in sweat pants or gym shorts, and forget the accoutrements. Save the kickline, lose the props.

Superintendents of school systems have expressed worries about the status of "powder-puff" football games, where the girls dress in the boys' football uniforms and the boys wear the cheerleading outfits, plus nerf balls or balloons. I have yet to hear about girls who stuff socks down their pants, in order to more accurately imitate the male anatomy. Is it that the girls aren't "allowed" to be this raunchy or they are too "polite or repressed" (I highly doubt it) to do so. My suggestion to these superintendents is to continue with the event, just leave out the props (see Chapter 5 for a discussion of raunchy behaviors by students and the ways in which school officials mete out discriminatory punishments for the same behaviors).

There are some who advocate that any and all "cross-dressing" in schools should be outlawed, but I am opposed to such a sweeping rule. What would happen to performances of *South Pacific*, Shakespeare, Kabuki theater or original Greek tragedy? Such a rule would lead down the slippery road to more censorship in the subculture of schools that are already not very friendly to free expression and other rights guaranteed in the Bill of Rights.

USE OF TITLE IX FOR LANGUAGE PURIFICATION

I have noticed that there is a rising tide of attempts to use federal law, namely, Title IX, as a language-purification law: school personnel and parents want to use it to purge dirty words from students' vocabulary; and the right wing, especially Christian fundamentalists, are trying to use it as a way to challenge sex and AIDS education. For example, in Massachusetts, some parents, backed by the Rutherford Institute, a Christian legal organization based in Fredericksburg, Virginia, tried to use federal law Title IX to sue the Chelmsford, Massachusetts, school district for conducting an AIDS education assembly in the high school (Brelis, 1993; *Brown v. Hot, Sexy and Safer*, 1995). There are also certain factions of extremists (who are often women) who label anything that they find offensive, raunchy, or vulgar as sexual harassment. In some circles, the following statement is viewed as sexual harassment, no matter the age of the speakers: "I see London, I see France, I see Susie's underpants" (S. Ferraro, personal communication, fall 1994).

It all may add up to a further abrogation of the First Amendment in schools. And, in the midst of this reduction of First Amendment rights, gender matters—that is to say, depending on the gender of the speaker/actor, more or less speech is available, more or less First Amendment rights prevail.

We now turn our attention to what I consider to be the gendered (i.e., discriminatory) application of First Amendment rights to students.

5

When Girls Get Raunchy: A Gendered Application of the First Amendment

THE AXIOM seems to be that when boys do something off-color or raunchy, it is often begrudgingly tolerated and considered as part of "school culture," in other words, transformed into "boy culture equals the rest of our (school) culture." However, as soon as girls conduct their own version of the activity or the prank, the activity gets censored, or at least "noticed" by the authorities, and the punishment toward the girls is often harsher than that the boys may receive. In this chapter I will explore several situations of differential treatment by school administrators of conduct they deem to be filled either with sexual innuendo or raunchiness; the gender of the students involved seems to play a pivotal role.

I first came to notice this gender disparity in the treatment of raunchy pranks when one occurred in my own backyard. It had been the longstanding tradition in this upper-middle-class suburb of Boston that senior boys, once they had graduated, would streak naked, with paper bags on their heads, by the glass windows of the cafeteria during lunch period while the students from Grades 9 to 11 were eating lunch. In 1993, the graduating senior girls engaged in this same stunt, without the boys.

Upon this new development, the guidance counselors called the Center for Research on Women, requesting one of us to speak with the girls. When I was asked, I refused outright, pointing out the sexism of their request, and inquired why the boys wouldn't be included in this little chat: If it was bad

74

for the girls to do this prank, why was it not also inappropriate for boys? The answer I received was that it was "more dangerous" for the girls. I disagreed, pointing out the safety features that were built into the prank: It occurred in daylight; the girls were in a group; and it was conducted on public property. Unfortunately, I have no knowledge of what happened to the girls or even if the tradition continues; this is hardly the material covered by this town's local newspaper.

Another incident in Andover, Massachusetts: a young woman was suspended for wearing a T-shirt of the rock group White Zombies, which portrays two fully clothed, large-breasted cartoon versions of women; it was a very colorful, chaotic-looking T-shirt. The female assistant principal explained that she found this illustration to be offensive, even though the young woman, as she was arguing her case, pointed out to the administrator that she, the girl, was large breasted. "Does this make me offensive," she inquired of the administrator? "Do you want me to get a breast reduction?" (Downes, 1994; Gladfelter, 1994; Staruk, 1994).

After being suspended, this senior who was on the honor roll, albeit one who is "in your face," returned to school property, standing on a rock outside that the students refer to as "protest rock." There she stood, waving her bra and ultimately putting it on over her T-shirt (sort of Madonna-like, where the bra is worn on the outside of clothes). Then three police cars and one motorcycle unit arrived, sirens blaring, to arrest her for disturbing the peace and creating a public nuisance. She was handcuffed and put in jail for three hours, until the Massachusetts chapter of the American Civil Liberties Union bailed her out and continued to represent her in court. Letters of support came in from MTV, Geffen Records, and the rock group, White Zombies. The young woman, Yvonne Nicoletti, summarized the incident this way: "I was arrested for standing up for my identity, freedom of expression and breast size" (Gladfelter, 1994, p. 1).

A different and recent variation on what happens to girls who engage in raunchy behavior occurred in Southlake, Texas, in February 1997. Two (female) cheerleaders and four baseball (male) players were caught "mooning" one another from their cars. At first, all received identical punishments (3-day suspensions), but the consequences soon dramatically diverged: the baseball players were suspended for three games, but the cheerleaders were removed from the squad permanently ("Students Blue over 'Mooning,'" 1997).

The parents of the girls protested the differences in the penalties, asserting that their daughters were the victims of a double standard that is discriminatory. However, the school officials asserted their claim that "the punishment was appropriate because the cheerleaders must sign an agreement acknowledging that they can be kicked off the squad if they are involved in a serious disciplinary incident or engage in 'unladylike' behavior" ("Students Blue over 'Mooning,'" 1997, p. 4).

Although I am no fan of mooning whether from a moving car or a stationary position, I agree with the parents of the girls that the school delivered gender-discriminatory punishments. I am also concerned about the application of the term *unladylike*, with its rather vague and ambiguous features. Moreover, whatever happened to the axiom that playing sports developed character for boys—wouldn't this conduct be grounds enough to remove those boys from the privilege of playing sports? Sexist assumptions and implications of privilege ooze from this example.

In the next section, I will explore in depth a situation that rocked a town in Iowa and provides an in-depth example of disparity in the treatment of male and female raunchiness by school administrators.

HOOTERS AND COCKS T-SHIRTS IN AMES, IOWA

For more than a year, some boys in a middle school in Ames, Iowa, wore "Hooters" T-shirts—owl eyes peer out from the letter *O*, falling strategically around the nipple area, with the slogan "More than a mouthful" placed sometimes on the back, sometimes on front, of the T-shirt. In response, a group of eighth-grade girls decided to create a parallel parody and after some friendly adult (fathers and male teachers) input, created a T-shirt with the slogan "Cocks. Nothing to crow about."

However, by the time these T-shirts were rolling off the presses, both the Hooters and Cocks T-shirts had been banned by the principal. That was not the outcome that the girls wanted. In the words of Sarah Hegland, one of the leaders, "We wanted the hooters shirts to be socially unacceptable rather than legally unacceptable" (Basu, 1994, p. 11A).

Despite the threat of suspension, about 20 students wore their Cocks T-shirts to school on a particular day. Most students did not make it to their first-period class in these shirts—they were met at the front door and told to turn the shirts inside out. Most complied—four did not and were suspended (three boys and one girl). The leaders, Erin Rollenhagen and Sarah Hegland, joined a group of other girls in the principal's office to discuss the issues implicit in this episode. As Erin told me in an interview in October 1995, "Sarah and I felt it was our job to negotiate to get some positive outcomes." They repeated what they had articulated in an earlier letter to the principal—they wanted a public forum on the two issues embedded in this episode, free speech and sexism.

They got their public forum, and about 300 people attended, including the national director of the American Civil Liberties Union, Ira Glasser, who happened to be in Ames at the same time. Their story made the local and national press (Basu, 1994a; Burns, 1994; Luthro, 1994; National ACLU Director Enters Iowa School Dispute, 1994; O'Donnell, 1994; Palmer, 1994). Erin wrote an article published in *Seventeen* magazine (Rollenhagen, 1994), but I prefer to quote from her original manuscript, which she provided to me, rather than the version that was published in *Seventeen*:

> It's true, no major school policy changes were made, but there were some other changes. At least for a while, people talked and thought about sexism. A lot of us really needed this controversy to remind us that we do have the right to demand respect for ourselves. Unfortunately, some people still didn't get the point. Our local paper ran an editorial calling our shirts "silly" and "stupid, perhaps." . . . The bottom line is: there are jerks out there who already have and will continue to tell women that we are inferior, helpless sex objects.

Erin's words hold relevance to another T-shirt case, this time one that ended up in federal courts.

WHEN THE SHIRT HITS THE FAN: COED NAKED T-SHIRTS ENTER THE U.S. DISTRICT COURT

Coed Naked T-Shirts, a New Hampshire company with a booming business, has made major inroads into student culture, found both in secondary schools and universities. Some of the statements found on T-shirts include:

> "coed naked tennis—it's in, it's out, it's over."
> "coed naked truck driving—if you truck too fast, you'll lose your load."
> "coed naked soccer—get your kicks in the grass."
> "coed naked field hockey—make a pass in the grass."
> "coed naked international soccer—try to score in every country."
> "coed naked fire-fighting—find them hot, leave them wet."
> "coed naked law enforcement—up against the wall and spread 'em."
> "coed naked gambling—lay them on the table."
> "coed naked auto-racing—lapping the competition."
> "coed naked lacrosse—ruff and tuff in the buff."
> "coed naked billiards—get felt on the table."

Some schools ban these (in fact, one Massachusetts middle school principal told me that he bans them because they promote "illegal" activity. When I asked what that was, he told me, "Being naked in public"), some allow them, and one school district found itself in federal court for censoring one of these T-shirts (*Pyle v. The South Hadley School Committee*, 1994).

In March 1993, Jeffrey Pyle wore a "Coed Naked Band: Do it to the rhythm" T-shirt to South Hadley (MA) High School, a gift to him, a member of the band, from his mother. His physical education teacher found it to be unacceptable, and warned him not to wear it again, saying that this T-shirt targeted or harassed a person because of race, sex, religion, or sexual orientation. Even though no girls or boys complained about this T-shirt—this teacher felt that a hostile environment was created (or, might be created) by this T-shirt. As the son of a constitutional law professor at Mt. Holyoke College and a librarian, Jeffrey knew and asserted his First Amendment rights, writing in a letter to his acting principal that he planned to wear it again, that he and other students, both boys and girls, had worn these shirts in the past and had not received any complaints. He also included in his letter to the acting principal: "Of course, if any of my shirts were to cause a genuine disruption, I would change it immediately." Jeffrey received no reply from the school administrator.

Suffice it to say, Jeffrey wore the T-shirt again, and his physical education teacher asked him to change it. Jeffrey refused, and was given three detentions and sent to the office. The acting principal decided to bring the matter to the school board, and the detention was held in abeyance until that future meeting. In the meantime, Jeffrey wore two other T-shirts with sexual innuendos: one depicted two men in naval uniform kissing each other with the tag line "Read my lips"; the second T-shirt used the official centennial slogan for Smith College, "A century with women on top." Neither shirt prompted any objections from school personnel.

Several school board meetings came and went, at which time different proposals were considered regarding amendments to the existing dress code. The amendments that passed on May 3, 1993, were the following:

> Students are not to wear clothing that: (1) has comments or designs that are obscene, lewd or vulgar; (2) is directed toward or intended to harass, threaten, intimidate or demean an individual or group of individuals because of sex, color, race, religion, handicap, national origin or sexual orientation; (3) advertises alcoholic beverages, tobacco products, or illegal drugs; (4) Clothing expressing political views is allowed as long as the views are not expressed in a lewd, obscene or vulgar manner. (*Pyle v. South Hadley School Committee*, 1994, pp. 10-11).

The next day, Jeffrey wore "Coed Naked Civil Liberties: Do it to the Amendments." His younger brother Jonathan wore "See Dick drink. See Dick drive. See Dick die. Don't be a dick." Both boys, refusing to remove their T-shirts, were sent home. As the school board was hearing arguments from legal counsel, Jonathan wore this T-shirt: "Coed naked gerbils: Some people will censor anything." This T-shirt was found to be permissible. Later, he wore "Coed naked censorship: They do it in South Hadley." The principal said that this T-shirt did not violate the dress code. Nor did the official Smith College centennial T-shirt: "Smith College. A century of women on top."

To summarize, sexual innuendos were considered objectionable, but T-shirts that sexually targeted a particular gender, such as the two men French-kissing or the Smith College one—were permissible. As the person who would eventually serve as the expert witness on behalf of Jeffrey and Jonathan, I was perplexed by the rather arbitrary and capricious dress code, but I was even more curious about what the school officials considered sexually charged as opposed to sexually targeted. I dare say schools are more sensitive to and uptight about "sexually charged" than "sexually targeted."

Expert Witness Testimony

Jeffrey, Jonathan, and their family decided to file a First Amendment lawsuit in U.S. Federal Court. As the expert witness serving on behalf of the young men and their counsel, the Massachusetts American Civil Liberties Union, my testimony focused on the lessons that can be derived from the two national surveys on sexual harassment (the *Seventeen* magazine survey, 1993; and the Harris poll, 1993). First of all, I testified to the fact that in neither survey were T-shirts identified as sources of sexual harassment. Certainly, graffiti or notes that target a particular individual or gender were considered by students to be sexual harassment. But sexual innuendo in a nontargeted manner—where no one gender or individual is targeted—was not seen by kids as a form of sexual harassment.

Moreover, I testified to the fact that young women are not passive in the face of what they consider to be sexual harassment: they tell the ha-rasser, tell their friends, throw stuff at the harasser, hit the harasser, tell their parents, and tell school officials. Or they walk away. Therefore, neither judges nor school personnel can claim that they are speaking for the voice-less, passive girls, because girls are often neither! School personnel seemed to have wanted to issue a kind of "prior restraint"—to protect the girls and censor the T-shirts before anyone objected. Such censorship would seem to be predicated upon the assumption that girls need protection from words because girls are fragile and vulnerable. But, as the survey results reveal, girls are not passive and they are not voiceless. A curious footnote regard-ing the popularity of the Coed Naked T-shirts is that they were often worn by girls. According to the manufacturer, six outlets in western Massachu-setts sold 13,000 of the shirts in 1992, of which 80% were purchased by females (C. Pyle, 1994).

The Various Courts' Decisions

Federal District Court Judge Ponsor issued a split decision, which while dismissing the charge of sexual harassment, constrained the First Amendment. Judge Ponsor ruled that the South Hadley ban on clothing "that harasses, threatens, intimidates or demeans certain individuals or groups" will be enjoined; in other words, struck down. However, "the court will deny the (plaintiff's) motion for injunctive relief directed at the two t-shirts themselves and at that portion of the dress code forbidding clothing that is 'obscene, profane, lewd or vulgar'" (*Pyle v. South Hadley School Committee*, 1994, p. 3).

Not surprisingly, the decision was appealed to the circuit court, and in April 1995, the case was heard in the U.S. Court of Appeals for the First Circuit in Boston. In June of 1995, the First Circuit asked for a ruling from the Supreme Judicial Court of Massachusetts regarding student expression, including restrictions on dress. The case was argued in the Supreme Judicial Court of Massachusetts in February of 1996, and on July 25, 1996, the Supreme Judicial Court reaffirmed the rights of students. At least in Massachusetts, students still have First Amendment rights, and until their clothing (which is a form of symbolic speech) actually produces a disruption, censorship cannot be invoked on the pretext that such speech might cause a disruption. It was a great victory for civil libertarians, for students, and for free speech (Bai, 1996).

Yet, larger questions remain hanging and will likely reoccur: Is this case just a different version of the sexist application of the First Amendment—when girls are the imagined aggrieved party as well as when girls engage in a raunchy activity or prank, there is a crackdown on speech or symbolic speech from school authorities?

At this point, words from one of the young men plaintiffs in this case, Jeffrey Pyle, offers some needed insights into the larger implications of this case. Jeffrey knows well of girls' abilities to give voice to their interests and concerns:

> They [a coalition of forces and groups] want to deprive young people, but mostly girls, of the freedom to joke about sex without being misunderstood—a right we thought girls had won in the sexual revolution of the 1960's and 1970's. But they want to take that right away from girls by treating them as putative victims and boys as inherent predators. . . .
>
> This . . . stereotypes and demeans both sexes. It says that girls cannot be expected to stand up to messages that really are offensive to them, that they aren't as equal as they thought they were when they bought most of the "coed naked" shirts. (J. Pyle, 1994, p. 7)

Jeffrey's words provide an analysis that is strikingly similar to the analysis offered by Erin: Both young people understand historical struggle and context, victories always tempered over time by forces of slippage and regression. Simultaneously, both young people seem able to keep a sense of perspective and maintain common sense. Unfortunately, the double standard that both of these astute observers point to have been institutionalized in several decisions that have been rendered by the courts or the Office for Civil Rights.

Imagine the ways in which the discourse about gender roles and sexual harassment would be informed and transformed if school classrooms were to engage in cross-talk and challenges as posed by Jeffrey and Erin. Their voices, if expressed, and not suppressed or demonized in the classroom, would go a long way to minimizing and altering the often flat and didactic manner in which the conversations about gender and sexual harassment is pursued in schools. In an interview before the final decision was rendered in July 1996, Jeffrey stated that he felt that the T-shirt issue could have "been resolved through Socratic dialogue rather than legal action. You can negotiate without coercion" (Davis, 1996, p. 28; *Jeffrey J. Pyle and another v. School Committee of South Hadley and others*, 1996).

Interestingly, the controversy aroused by this case continues among law and education professors (Fossey & DeMitchell, 1997; Murray & Stein, 1997; Pyle & Pyle, 1997), and led at least one Pyle brother into law school.

CONCLUSION

Sexism remains a fundamental part of school culture. When girls act raunchy, whether by acting alone, in groups with other girls, or as compatriots with boys, their actions and participation are deemed inappropriate.

On the other hand, when the adults perceive girls to be the targets of sexual harassment by their peers, the urge is to protect them and punish the harassers in what might be a rush to judgment by the adults. However, when boys get harassed or hazed, the conduct is viewed as just play, horsing around, a rite of passage into manhood, and even a honor (see Chapter 2 for discussion of several cases on this very point). I believe that this double standard is apparent to the students and has consequences—the boys feel abandoned by the adults, while at the same time, develop hostility toward sexual-harassment-prevention efforts, and maybe even toward their female peers. I dare say that their hostility at adult hypocrisy is understandable and deserved.

Sexism also shows up in the area of free expression: Free expression (speech and symbolic speech) rights in schools are applied and responded to differentially by gender. When boys do it, the First Amendment is often invoked, and they are not censored, unless their conduct is labeled sexual harassment (as with the Pyle T-shirt case). Yet, when the girls act in a manner that is regarded as off-color, unconventional, or unladylike, as with all the examples provided in this chapter, their conduct gets noticed, censored, and punished—they are seen as acting in a sex-role-inappropriate manner. Although their behaviors are usually not labeled as sexual harassment, the girls are exploding sex role stereotypes and their behaviors are regarded as disruptive.

Sadly, the First Amendment rights of students are not alive or well in K–12 schools. First Amendment rights have been diminished as many pranks and activities have been labeled or mislabeled as sexual harassment—they might be sexist, even offensive, and sexually charged. But are they sexual harassment?

In the short run, we might try to expand the vocabulary of students and school personnel alike to move us beyond the misapplication and overapplication of the expression *sexual harassment*, and the deeper conceptual confusion between those events, activities, and speech that are sexually charged as compared with those that are sexually hostile and intimidating. The rush to judgment to label sexist conduct as sexual harassment may in fact be reduced once we teach the broader concept and definitions of sex discrimination. Besides expanding vocabulary, additional benefits might include the discovery and elimination of sexually discriminatory practices—in athletic budgets, in the curriculum, and in personnel practices.

The last time I checked, the Constitution still applies to girls. We need to remind our schools to apply the Bill of Rights, at least what is left of it, for students, including the girls, too, even when they act raunchy.

6

Slippery Justice

W<small>HEN THE COURTS</small> around the country disagree with one another or are reluctant to provide clarity, and when school administrators are confused and having panic attacks because of their fear of lawsuits and bad publicity, educators need to keep vigilant about the ways that they may overapply and misapply sexual harassment to situations and events that do not warrant such a characterization. One of the consequences of an overapplication and misapplication is to be found in the realm of punishments and justice in the schoolhouse.

There is a new trend afoot, that of draconian measures imposed upon students by school personnel, induced most likely by a fear of lawsuits against school districts. Harsh penalties are meted out to the offenders while at the same time, targets of sexual harassment are often hung out to dry—required to solve the problem and confront the harasser, often on their own. What could school officials be thinking? This chapter will look at the actions and reactions of school personnel: some absurd, some extreme, others purporting to be empowering, all dispensed in the schoolhouse in the name of justice.

Incidents of sexual harassment have been typically handled by school personnel in arbitrary, rigid, or uninspired ways—ranging from reading students the riot act, to looking the other way, to imposing standards that in some cases are more strict than those in our courts. Oftentimes the discipline consists of little more than "a wink and a nod" scolding in the principal's office. Respondents to our 1992 *Seventeen* magazine survey on sexual harassment noted the dismissive way in which their appeals for help were regarded and the cavalier manner in which the harassers were treated:

> I feel that school administration needs to view this as a serious problem. In my particular case, I was receiving comments pertaining to sexual parts of my body,

and being asked to respond to sexually explicit jokes. This went on for over 6 months. I was fed up. After reporting this *three* times to the school administration, I was told that these boys were "flirting" and had a "crush" on me. I was disgusted with the actions of the administration. They told me they would give the boys a strict warning. I saw them do it. I don't think *asking* someone to stop harassing another person is a strict warning. The worse part of the whole thing, is that they gave them the same "warning" on three different occasions. The harassing never stopped and I was humiliated; I'm scared. If you can't feel comfortable at school, how can you get a good education? Something has got to change. (14-years-old, White, Illinois) (Stein, Marshall, & Tropp, 1993, p. 10A)

When my parents called the principal about two boys who were harassing me, he took it seriously enough to call their parents, and the harassment from those particular boys stopped. What makes me mad is that there were teachers who knew about the problem before my parents called the principal, but didn't do anything to stop it. I think that if they had done something earlier, the problem wouldn't have gotten as bad as it did. (15-years-old, White, California) (p. 10A)

I've been harassed in FRONT of teachers and hall monitors, maybe even a janitor or two, and certainly other students, NONE OF WHOM took any action. They probably dismissed it as flirting, or maybe they were just ignorant and didn't care. (14-years-old, White, New York) (p. 3A)

PERVERSIONS OF JUSTICE

When forced to acknowledge that sexual harassment has landed in their building, school officials often impose antidemocratic policies upon the school community. Unfortunately, at times these measures have been imposed for students' out-of-school conduct, and at other times, school administrators have simply resorted to calling in the police to handle these problems.

Draconian Approaches

School officials have often used draconian approaches in an attempt to regulate both school-based as well as out-of-school conduct. An absurd example of the former occurred in January 1995 in the Millis, Massachusetts, school district, when it banned hand-holding, hugging, and other affectionate physical contact between students on school grounds (Moroney, 1995). This was not the standard prohibition of "no public displays of affection," but rather an attempt to rectify months of neglect by school administrators who had minimized allegations of sexual assault of 11 females by a star football player.

This severe measure actually was in keeping with the rigidity and denial that had been manifested by several of the school administrators who had done their best to ignore the allegations of sexual assault (a charge to which the young man later pleaded guilty to one count of statutory rape and several counts of assault, for which he earned a 18-month prison sentence). Ironically, both approaches—denial of the allegations on the one hand, and on the other hand, the ban on hand-holding—may be indicative of the panic that has set in because of the threat of lawsuits (Moroney, 1995; Pitsch, 1995). After much derision and ridicule in the press and by the educational community, the Millis School District reconsidered the ban on hand-holding.

Another arena of the draconian reach is for school administrators to attempt to police the behaviors between students that occur beyond the school day and off school grounds. Many schools for years have attempted to regulate the off-campus behaviors of athletes beyond the season in which they play school-sponsored sports. A further development of this trend is to extend the reach of sanctions on off-campus student conduct. A particularly troubling example is one that involved a 13-year-old boy in Liverpool, New York, who left a message that was described as partly obscene and partly goofy on the phone answering machine of a female classmate (Lewin, 1998). The message combined childlike comments such as "I feed you ice" along "with graphic sexual threats about shoving a Remington semiautomatic and a box of cornflakes into her private parts" (p. 23).

School officials maintain that they were compelled to suspend the offending student for a large portion of the school year because of their interpretation of federal antidiscrimination law as requiring them to maintain an atmosphere that is not sexually hostile. There are other examples beyond the scope of this chapter and this book that unfortunately provide evidence of overzealous school officials who have monitored and evaluated student behavior at parties in private homes, at shopping malls, on the Internet from home computers, and on the streets. In some cases, the courts have upheld the rights of school administrators to punish students for their out-of-school conduct, and in other cases, the courts have reversed the decisions of the schools, and have awarded damages to the students ("ACLU Sues MO School over Student's Personal Web Site," 1998).

Criminalizing the Conduct

Another common overreaction that administrators seem to gravitate toward is to invite the police into the schools to teach about sexual assault and harassment or to investigate allegations of sexual harassment. Not trained as educators, the police officers have a classroom style that is frequently didactic and one dimensional, and their mere presence can escalate the conversation and investigation to one of criminality, as opposed to allowing the allegations (if warranted) to remain in the civil domain.

At other times, school officials may tell the student or her or his family making the initial complaint that until the police complete their investigation, the school will not take a stand. Such a cop-out by the school officials is reprehensible on several accounts: We do not live in a police state—affairs of the school, particularly when criminal conduct is not an issue, should be handled by school officials and not turned over to the police, merely as a convenience or as a way to teach the students a lesson. Moreover, by calling in the police, the school administrators have abdicated their responsibility for resolving the problem; it is as if they have just thrown up their hands in exasperation, and called in the cavalry.

In part, the trend of school administrators to call in the police for matters of sexual harassment may be a result of child-abuse reporting laws, which require school officials to call the proper state agency and authorities. After years of school officials' mistakenly thinking that they had jurisdiction for investigations of alleged child abuse, they have come to rely on outsiders for such investigations. This may in part explain the reasons why they often call in the police to investigate allegations of sexual harassment.

"STUDENT EMPOWERMENT" APPROACHES

An alternative to the draconian approach are the student empowerment approaches, which in some cases amount to students' being stranded and forced to handle the complaints on their own.

Peer Mediation

An entirely different approach to resolving sexual harassment disputes is predicated on a totally opposite conception of student autonomy. This version of resolution is to require disputing students to face off with each other as a pair or sometimes in the presence of a student-peer mediator. This technique, whether framed in the trendy vernacular of "peer mediation" or "alternative dispute resolution" or seen as an opportunity for student empowerment or for reclaiming one's voice can be misused when it is used as a replacement for punishment of the harassing student, or when students are forced to go into mediation (which should always be a voluntary act on the part of each disputant).

In some cases, this misapplication of mediation can end up buying the school district a lawsuit. This was the situation in December 1992 at Blair High School in Silver Springs, Maryland (Montgomery County), where an assistant principal required a girl to confront her male attacker, alone in a room. This conversation ultimately resulted in a screaming match between the girl and the boy, and her parents filed a lawsuit against the school district (Peller, 1993; Sherrod, 1993, 1994; Sullivan, 1993). In the December 1993 letter of agreement signed by Superintendent Paul L. Vance with the U.S. Department of Education's Office for Civil Rights, the school district stated that it will no longer "require or direct a complainant to attend a face to face meeting, or confront in any way, the alleged harasser in a complaint of sexual harassment" (Montgomery County Public Schools, 1993).

Write a Letter to the Harasser

Another technique that has gained popularity with school personnel is to have the target/victim of sexual harassment write a letter to the harasser. First developed by Mary Rowe (1981), special assistant to the president at the Massachusetts Institute of Technology and a professor at the Sloan School of Management, this technique was later adapted by Dr. Rowe and me for application with high school students in the 1982 Massachusetts Department of Education curriculum, *Who's Hurt and Who's Liable.*

The original assumptions underlying the rationale of sending a letter to the harasser have merit and include the following (Stein, 1993a):

- It is an active response to the sexual harassment by the target.
- It changes the balance of power: the target of the sexual harassment becomes proactive and the harasser is placed in a "receiver" role.
- It shows the harasser there are consequences to these behaviors that live beyond the time of the incident.
- It catches the harasser alone. The letter should be given to the harasser by the target (if she or he chooses) in the presence of an adult staff member, preferably in the privacy of the adult staff member's office. If the target would prefer not to be present, then the alleged harasser should be handed the letter in private by the adult.
- The letter, given to the harasser in an adult's office, forces the harasser to face up to behaviors in a different context from the one in which the harassment was committed.
- It allows the target to feel safe; the harasser is confronted, yet not in a face-to-face situation.
- The letter serves a legal purpose by documenting the incident, the specific behaviors, the presence of witnesses, and the target's feelings. It also serves to give the harasser "fair warning" to stop.
- It helps to contain the incident of sexual harassment among a small group of people—the target, the adult advocate, and the alleged harasser.

This letter-writing tactic has proven to be transferable to peer-to-peer sexual harassment cases in schools (Lydiard, 1993). With the collaboration of an adult trained in this technique, writing a letter to the harasser becomes a step toward taking some control over situations that often cause depression, fear, bewilderment, anxiety, and anger in the target of the harassment. The act of letter writing is positive and even therapeutic because it is proactive.

Cooperation with a school staff member accomplishes other important goals: The target speaks to someone about the incident and his or her feelings; the incident is documented; and only a small group of people are involved in discussing the incident, thus maintaining the privacy rights of both the alleged harasser and the victim/subject.

While the letter-writing technique is a proactive response for the target and one that respects the privacy rights of the accused, unfortunately it does not mitigate the negative collective learning that has already occurred among the bystanders who witnessed or heard about the sexual harassment incident. The hidden curriculum of sexual harassment that affects the whole school community is still not addressed by this technique (Stein, 1993a).

For that reason letter writing should in no way be seen as a strategy to prevent or eliminate sexual harassment in general; it will not take the place of strategies such as training programs, support groups, discipline codes, and grievance procedures. A further limitation of this technique is quite obvious—in order to send a letter to the harasser, the target must know the perpetrator, or at least be able to identify the harasser. It would be rather difficult to implement this letter-writing tactic in response to notes or group catcalls.

Unfortunately, the "write a letter to the harasser" technique has become formulaic, overvalorized, overused, and glorified. Oftentimes this panacea is forced upon a target of sexual harassment, including times when criminal conduct is alleged to have taken place. Letter writing should belong in the realm of options from which the target can chose. Most egregiously, this technique places the burden of responsibility upon the target of the harassment, and not upon the school personnel whose responsibility it is to create a school environment that is free from sexual harassment. This bears repeating: It is not the responsibility of the target to solve the problem of sexual harassment in schools.

The Courtroom in the Classroom

For other educators, the course of justice for adjudicating sexual harassment conflicts has consisted of efforts to replicate the courtroom in the schoolhouse. Rights of citizens as guaranteed by the U.S. Constitution—that of a trial by a jury of one's peers and for the accused to confront his or her accuser—have been imported into disciplinary proceedings for sexual harassment accusations. Like it or not, the courts have made distinctions between the rights of citizens and those of minor students in schools, resulting in fewer rights in the schoolhouse. But, somehow, the courtroom standard seems to be invoked only for sexual harassment disputes—and not for other altercations, where administrators typically act swiftly and unequivocally. Somehow sexual harassment allegations are regarded as an opportunity for a consensus-building moment between the disputants or as an opportunity whose outcome should be determined by a popular vote of representatives of the student body. This double standard of treatment (sexual harassment disputes vs. other kinds of disputes) needs to be disbanded.

Consider the classic example of a popular student (often an athlete) accused of sexual harassment or sexual assault. The student who has come forward with this charge is not only blamed for having brought the behavior upon herself, but she is treated as a pariah for jeopardizing the reputation of a popular boy and also as a traitor to the whole school for damaging its reputation. Imagine the outcome if this case were to be put before a tribunal of one's peers—the popular boy would probably win, hands down. The bitter lessons left in the aftermath might give license, if not to him, then maybe to others, that they, too, could operate with impunity.

This was the exact plot of a CBS after-school special, *Sexual Considerations*, that aired on October 20, 1992, and again in 1995. Written by Pamela Douglass and produced by Susan Rohrer, from the NorthStar Entertainment Group in Virginia Beach, Virginia, the plot involved the popular male editor of the school newspaper who offered a plum reporting assignment to a young woman student reporter if she would comply with his sexual requests. She wouldn't, she complained to adult advisors, she was tried by a student tribunal—and she was not believed. This plot line dealt the issue of sexual harassment multiple blows: that quid pro quo sexual harassment occurs among students, that adults can only recite the workplace definition of sexual harassment when they realize that sexual harassment is occurring among the students in school, and that a trial by one's peers is a popularity contest. The final message of this television show may be that speaking up is a futile act, and that adults are no help.

TEMPORARY RESTRAINING ORDERS

Temporary restraining orders (TROs), or civil orders of protection, have also found their way into the schoolhouse. Although these are typically used for adults (married or cohabiting) in abusive relationships, 13 states have deemed non-cohabitating minors to be eligible for temporary restraining orders (Alabama, Alaska, California, Colorado, Illinois, Massachusetts, Minnesota, New Hampshire, New Mexico, North Dakota, Oklahoma, Pennsylvania, and West Virginia) (Levesque, 1997) (see Conclusion). For example, in Massachusetts as of January 1991, people involved in "significant dating relationships" were added to the list of those qualified for temporary restraining orders (Massachusetts General Laws, 1991), to protect them from harm (Hohler, 1992, 1993; Ingrassia et al., 1993; Kowalczyk, 1993; Locy, 1994).

Although a temporary restraining order may act to symbolically acknowledge the violence that exists in relationships, controversy exists over the value of obtaining one. It is widely considered that a woman's life is in greatest danger when she obtains a TRO against an abuser. However, for the great majority of adolescents in abusive relationships, this is a moot point because they cannot get civil or criminal protections of any sort (Levesque, 1997). Even in those 13 states where they are permitted to obtain this safeguard, implementing these orders of protections takes considerable effort on the part of the school administrators and teachers.

Imagine if the female student in the case depicted in the above television scenario had obtained a TRO; or imagine other nonfictional situations wherein a teenage couple ends their dating relationship or one person pursues (or stalks) another who is not interested in having a close, personal relationship—think of the awkward position of school administrators who have to enforce restraining orders in their buildings. In the closed environment of the school community, where students mingle informally in hallways, the cafeteria, and the parking lot, it may seem insurmountable to expect that restraining orders can be enforced.

Yet, school administrators must make extra efforts to do so. In some states, the civil rights division of the attorney general's office offers guidelines for administrators who find themselves needing to assist in the implementation of an order of protection. Irrespective of the existence of a civil order of protection between two students, schools might create their own version of a stay-away or temporary restraining order, with its own time limitations, parental involvement, teacher oversight, and sanctions should the order be violated.

Given all the limitations of and obstacles to enforcing restraining orders in the outside world, we must remember that restraining orders are not panaceas—not for domestic violence, not for dating violence, and certainly not for sexual harassment in schools. Nonetheless, school administrators should take a proactive stance in confronting sexual violence and sexual harassment by developing their own version of TROs whether or not their state permits such safeguards for minors.

CONFIDENTIALITY

A further obstacle to justice in the schoolhouse revolves around matters of confidentiality. School administrators have either overinterpreted and over-applied requirements for confidentiality or they have abandoned investigations altogether when the complaining student has requested confidentiality.

On the one hand, requests for confidentiality often couched in the pro-verbial plea from a student to a teacher, "Please don't tell anyone that I told you this," is interpreted by the adult that they cannot proceed any further, let alone with a formal sexual harassment investigation. And, for many school personnel, that's as far as the complaint goes—nothing changes except that the student has aired her or his concerns.

At the very least, the adult hearing the complaint needs to inform the student that his or her wishes will be taken into consideration but that as an employee of the school district, she or he is required to take some steps, which would not necessarily reveal the original source. At the minimum, the adult who receives the complaint needs to pass it along to the Title IX coordinator or the school employee who is responsible for receiving complaints—that would be the only way to gauge whether there is a pattern of harassment developing. There needs to be a central repository for all sexual harassment complaints, even if students are encouraged to take their concerns, questions, and complaints to any adult in the building to whom they feel comfortable talking.

Moreover, for purposes of complying with Title IX, once the school "has notice" of a sexual harassment event, it is responsible for acting to remedy the harassment. The school employee who fails to report to the designated central repository person, be it the Title IX coordinator, principal, or super-intendent, may well indeed be incurring legal liability upon him- or herself and the entire school district.

On the other hand, there are instances when confidentiality requirements imposed through the Federal Educational Rights and Privacy Act (known as FERPA or the Buckley Amendment of 1974) are overapplied and overextended by school administrators. Indeed, this law imposes certain restrictions on a school's release of information contained in a student's educational record. However, complying with the Buckley Amendment doesn't mean that the administrator cannot inform the complaining student of the measures that have been taken in light of the complaint (U.S. Department of Education, 1997b).

Too often school administrators plead that they are restrained by the Buckley Amendment in such a way that they cannot report on the outcome of the complaint. Talk about an effective way to undercut and sabotage faith in the system of justice that schools are supposed to implement: If students are not told how their complaint has been handled, why should they believe that coming forward makes any difference at all? In order to build faith in whatever system of justice the school is delivering, there must be a feedback mechanism, at least to the complaining student and his or her faculty advisor.

One way for an administrator to both comply with the requirements of FERPA and to be able to report back to the complaining student and his or her faculty advisor is to require the harasser to reveal to the complainant (either in person or in writing, whichever the complainant prefers) the details of the discipline and punishment. This might entail having the harasser apologize to the complaining student, as well as reveal the disciplinary action(s) that have been taken.

Justice-making in the schoolhouse must encompass both a feedback mechanism and a concern for privacy for both the accused and the complainant. However, here is no reason why administrators should invoke FERPA as the reason for their silence. They may well be shooting themselves in the foot, or the mouth, as the case may be, if they choose total silence.

WHEN BOYS ARE THE TARGETS

Boys, too, are protected by federal law Title IX and may be targets of sexual harassment. However, very few have filed official complaints or lawsuits. When they have, the harassers have often been identified as other boys, and unfortunately, most cases have been dismissed by federal courts or denied for further investigation by the Office for Civil Rights of the U.S. Department of Education. No doubt there is a great deal of social pressure exerted on boys, both by their peers and by their elders, not to define unwanted sexual attention coming from the girls as "sexual harassment," or as "unwanted." However, there are some cases in which boys have been harassed for being homosexual, and in those few instances, the lawsuits and complaints have been settled on behalf of the boys (see Chapter 2).

The pretense of justice and equal protection under the law disappears when boys are the brunt of behaviors that are carried out in the name of initiation rites—as a new member to the school community or as a new member of a sports team. These rites of passage, in some circles called hazing or pledging, are viewed as an honor and a bonding mechanism to manhood or teamhood. The behaviors are often violent, even sexually violent, but are not viewed as violence, let alone as sexual harassment, and are often not condemned by adults (see Chapter 2).

The failure of the adults to notice and name this as inappropriate conduct has allowed the double standard to be reinvented: Boys get chastised and into trouble when they sexually harass girls, but when boys are targets of sexual harassment or hazing, the events are overlooked, excused as a rite of passage, or regarded as an honor. No wonder boys are resentful about the increased attention placed on sexual harassment; because of the hypocritical way in which sexual harassment is enforced, efforts to create gender equity and equal justice are undermined. If adults continue along this path, efforts to rid the schools of sexual harassment will be thwarted. In addition, along the way, justice is perverted and reduced.

WHERE DOES THIS LEAVE US?

First and foremost, sexual harassment should not be conceptualized as different from other violations of civil rights laws. Sexual harassment and the larger, related phenomenon of sex discrimination are part of our nation's laws on civil rights. Discrimination or harassment on the basis of sex should not be trivialized, ignored, or deemed so overwhelming that it resides in the realm of matters beyond the control of administrators. The argument sometimes used by school officials and their lawyers shows an acknowledgment of the pervasiveness of sexual harassment; yet in the next breath they claim that such pervasiveness means that they cannot do anything about curbing yet alone ending student-to-student sexual harassment. The general counsel for the National School Board Association, August Steinhilber, said in response to a court case that was decided against the student and in favor of the school district, "Districts cannot be held financially liable for every case in which students, who are private individuals, decide to act outside of the law. . . . It could be a serious drain on the finances of every school district" ("Court Absolves Schools of Student Sex Harassment," 1997, p. 3). One wonders if he and others would apply this logic in other areas of discrimination.

Moreover, educational personnel need to rid themselves of the fantasy that they can ignore the subject of sexual harassment until a problem emerges; by then, they will most likely have an incident on their hands that will be hard to contain. Because sexual harassment is a subject that is often in the news, such as the episodes in October 1996 with kissing 6- and 7-year-olds (see Chapter 3 for a discussion of sexual harassment in elementary schools), and also because it is a scary, titillating, and murky subject, people of all ages have lots of opinions about the issue. Feelings about all these topical and tangential events converge whenever a discrete incident of sexual harassment is under discussion at the school.

In the frenzy of the crisis, school personnel often rush to segment and isolate discussion of the problem to only those who are involved in the dispute, leaving most faculty as well as students in the dark. This practice, though maybe well intended, is foolhardy and may in fact backfire—often it is more difficult to diffuse the rumors that surround an episode of sexual harassment than it is to resolve the actual incident. Suffice it to say, the whole school community needs to be considered whenever sexual harassment incidents arise—bystanders and observers are at risk, too, of absorbing the bitter lessons of sexual harassment.

Above all, sexual harassment must be framed as a matter of creating a safe school and infusing a concern for social justice and democracy into the schools. Sexual harassment violates fundamental democratic principles, and the problem ought to be discussed in a way that highlights those principles. If schools are to be agents of democracy, helping to create citizens ready to participate in the democracy, we need to practice democracy in our schools. That means putting at the forefront conversations and lessons about social justice, including sexual harassment, and finding mechanisms for justice that are worthy of a democratic institution in a democratic society.

From Sexual Harassment to Sexual Violence in Schools: Disturbing Trends and Future Interventions

THE CONVERSATION among educators about the full range of sexual harassment and sexual violence in schools has only just begun. As school officials recognize that there are more acts of sexual harassment and sexual violence that take place in their buildings and on school grounds, it is not simply a matter of calling in the police to investigate the incidents as if they were simply restricted to alleged criminal violations. As more and more young people date at an earlier age; engage in, experience, or witness more sexual harassment and sexual violence in their schools; and suffer the consequences of watching partner/domestic abuse in their homes, educators are forced, with a vengeance, to recognize the existence of sexual violence in their schools.

As the previous chapters document, sexual harassment is everywhere in our schools. Certain incidents of sexual harassment that take place in school or during school-sponsored events are recognized as sexual violence (assault and rape, attempted or completed), and may be simultaneously pursued along several different legal channels: as a federal Title IX civil action against the school district and possibly a Fourteenth Amendment, equal protection clause (Section 1983) federal action against several individually named employees; as a state criminal action if the county or district attorney decides to pursue it; as state tort actions (negligence; inadequate or lack of supervision, etc.); and possibly as a violation of state child abuse laws. Within the range of behaviors that are considered to be sexual harassment fall some that are sexually violent, and much of sexual violence in schools is probably a form of sexual harassment. In this chapter I will review these few studies and surveys that provide us with information on sexual violence in K–12 schools.

RECOGNIZING THE PROBLEM

The first chapter of this book contained a letter from a 12-year-old girl to "Ask Beth," a syndicated teenage advice column. Beth's columns as well as surveys on sexual harassment and material gleaned from lawsuits discussed in the previous chapters of this book contain descriptions and statistics that reveal that students' appeals for help are often minimized and dismissed by teachers and administrators who choose to cast the purported assaults as playful or mutual or as a form of courtship.

Another letter to "Ask Beth" published on June 23, 1995, reveals again the neglect and denial that exists on the part of the adults:

> Dear Beth: My friend and I have been emotionally and physically hurt. We've been thrown into the boys' room and bruised from front to back. We talked to the teachers many times, but they say, "When I see them do it, I'll do something about it." They never see it so the boys keep doing it. We've been called bad names. We're only 11 and 12 and don't know what to do.
> Two girls in Henniker (NH) (Winship, 1995, p. 54)

It's not only advice columns that contain revelations about incidents of sexual assaults in schools; the hard-news sections of the newspaper also provide glimpses into the sexual violence that occurs in schools. Bathrooms seem to be the location for many of the sexual assaults, whether the schools are in Colorado, Florida, New York, or Boston ("Spate of Sexual Assaults in Bathrooms Raises Liability Questions," 1997). The assaults range from grabbing and stripping to attempted rape and rape. Buses also have been the sites of alleged assaults, and have been the subject of several lawsuits in the Fifth Circuit (*Rowinsky v. Bryan (TX) Independent School District*, 1996; *J. W. v. Bryan (TX) Independent School District*, 1997; and *Bowles et al. v. Floresville (TX) Independent School District*, 1993, 1994), none of which received rulings (or in some cases, even hearings) in favor of the plaintiffs. Despite unfavorable rulings from judges, common sense and experience allows us to agree that unfortunately school buses are not exactly sites of civilized behaviors, and some of those uncivilized behaviors include sexual assaults among the bus riders (i.e., children).

In the winter and spring of 1997–1998, there were a series of schoolyard shootings that shocked the nation. Girls were killed by boys in Jonesboro, Arkansas; Pearl, Mississippi; Norwalk, California; and Paducah, Kentucky. Yet the headlines in the nation's newspapers and magazines degendered these events, proclaiming "boys kill classmates." In addition, the responses from school and safety officials also ignored the deliberate gendered nature of these killings (Perlstein, 1998).

The conversation and the research into sexual violence in schools began with studies into dating violence among college students in the 1980s (Makepeace, 1981; Pirog-Good & Stets, 1989; and many other studies), followed by a few studies that surveyed high school students (Bergman, 1992; O'Keefe et al., 1986; Henton et al., 1983; Malik et al., 1997; Foshee, 1996). By the early 1990s, educators and researchers had begun to acknowledge the problem of teenage dating violence (Levy, 1991). However, those studies largely asked students about their relationships and conduct outside of school, the places where most dating violence manifested itself (parties, private homes, cars, the mall, and other public places), or either failed entirely to ask teenagers to specify the location of the dating violence. Questions about the spillover into school of violent dating relationships were not asked in research studies. Moreover, sexual harassment surveys, with the exception of that for Connecticut of 1995 (see Chapter 1), and the work of Fineran & Bennett (1995, 1998, 1999), to be reviewed later in this chapter, failed to probe into the current or former relationships between the harasser and the target. Finally, the National Crime Victimization Survey, a major source of crime victimization data in the United States, does inquire about what relationship, if any, existed between the perpetrator and victim at the time of the incident as well as the location where the incident occurred (including response options for "inside a school building" and "on school property"). Unfortunately, the survey uncovers too few incidents of rape and sexual assault to permit a detailed analysis by relationship and location (Bureau of Justice Statistics, 1997).

From *Hostile Hallways* (AAUW, 1993) and other sexual harassment surveys, a range of sexually violent behaviors can be identified, though the term *sexual violence* is never used or defined within the surveys. From examining the *Hostile Hallways* report, the only scientific/probability survey with a national sample, some of the behaviors identified (refer to Table 1.1) would be considered sexually violent largely because they fall into categories recognized as criminal conduct, whereas some other behaviors might be more open to interpretation about whether they were sexually violent, even though they are defined as sexual harassment (severe, pervasive, or repeated—see OCR definition and guidance in the Introduction). The following behaviors from Table 1.1 are ones that would most likely meet the standards of criminal conduct for sexual assault:

- Touched, grabbed, or pinched in a sexual way
- Had clothing pulled at in a sexual way
- Forced to kiss someone
- Had clothing pulled off or down
- Forced to do something sexual other than kissing

Taking the category "touched, grabbed, or pinched in a sexual way," since 65% of the girls reported experiencing these behaviors, then we can say that 65% of the girls experienced conduct that can be classified as sexual violence.

Although the many surveys on sexual harassment in schools reviewed in Chapter 1 allow us to look at incidents and events that are sexually violent, they fail to reveal anything about the relationship between the individuals involved. Unfortunately, on the other hand, most of the studies on dating violence do not provide information about the extent of the sexual violence that may occur in schools between the dating partners. Only a few studies, three articles by Fineran and Bennett (Bennett & Fineran, 1998; Fineran & Bennett, 1995, 1999), as well as an article by Molidor and Tolman (1998), have looked at the intersection of sexual harassment and dating violence by asking if the sexual harassment was coming from someone the target/victim was dating. Although the 1995 Connecticut sexual harassment survey (see Chapter 1) asked about the dating relationship, the survey was constructed in such a way as to not allow the extraction of this information from the answers provided by the respondents.

In large measure, we are left not knowing about the relationship between the individuals engaged in either sexual harassment or sexual violence in schools, except in the few studies to which we now turn our attention.

RESEARCH STUDIES ON SEXUAL VIOLENCE IN THE SCHOOLS

A major limitation of most of the research studies on teen dating violence is that the location for the violence is not specified. The review that follows considers only those studies that name school as a location for sexual violence between dating or formerly dating partners. Although little is known, it is very alarming. Reviewed are four studies that surveyed the behaviors of adolescents, and then a fifth study that focused on teachers' perceptions of dating violence in school.

Of the four studies, each was confined to one or two high schools, all in the Midwest; two studies were conducted in the mid-1980s (Roscoe & Callahan, 1985; Roscoe & Kelsey, 1986), and the other two in the mid-1990s (Bennett & Fineran, 1998; Molidor & Tolman, 1998). These four studies produced moderately substantiated conclusions about the existence of sexual violence in schools, albeit with convenience samples. The two studies conducted in the mid-1990s, one with an urban and suburban comparison (Bennett & Fineran, 1998) and the other in a large high school (Molidor & Tolman, 1998), both had populations that were racially diverse. Given the age of the other two studies from the 1980s, plus the fact that the sample was either entirely Caucasian or that the study was conducted in a religious school, I have decided to review only the two studies which are more recent, have a more racially diverse population, and are therefore more generalizable, despite their confinement to a few schools. A fifth study of teachers' perceptions of dating violence in school is also reviewed (Jasinski & West, 1997).

Bennett & Fineran (1998)

Bennett and Fineran surveyed 463 students from two midwestern high schools, one urban and one suburban. Both schools were racially diverse. The surveys were completed during a required English class in the urban school and during study halls in the suburban school. The survey asked primarily about sexual harassment in school but several of the questions asked about physical and sexual violence in school: "pressured me to do something sexual I did not want to do; attempted to physically hurt me (punch, kick, beat); and attempted to hurt me in a sexual way (attempted rape or rape)" (Fineran & Bennett, 1999). For each of these questions, students were asked to identify if they had been victimized by a schoolmate they did not know, a schoolmate they knew, or a dating or former dating partner. Students were also asked whether they had victimized any classmates or dating partners (Fineran & Bennett, 1999).

The final sample included 463 students (190 males and 273 females) who ranged in age from 14 to 20. The racial distribution was 27% Latino, 23% Caucasian, 34% African American, and 16% other. Thirty-two percent of the students reported that they had been the victims of severe physical violence (punched, kicked, or beaten), and 32% of the students reported perpetrating some form of severe physical aggression during the current school year. Twenty-two percent of the students reported experiencing sexual violence, and 6% reported perpetrating sexual violence. Fifteen percent of the students reported that they had experienced severe dating violence (sexual and physical violence combined), and 5% had perpetrated severe dating violence in the current school year.

Across the three relationships (schoolmate they did not know; schoolmate they knew; and a dating or former dating partner), boys were more likely to be the victims of physical violence and the perpetrators of physical and sexual violence. Girls were more likely to be the victims of dating violence and sexual violence and were more threatened and upset by the behaviors. For dating violence, 7 out of 10 cases were male to female.

Limitations of the study include a sample confined to two schools and a lack of information on students with disabilities or gay/lesbian students. No information was obtained on the severity of the injuries students experienced. A strength of this study is that it asked about behaviors that occurred at school.

Molidor & Tolman (1998)

This important study shows that dating violence is a form of school violence, and that a high percentage of the acts of dating violence occur on school grounds. As the authors state, "School is a dangerous place for young women" (Molidor & Tolman, 1998, p. 191).

Molidor and Tolman surveyed 736 students who attended a large midwestern high school. Students were surveyed in 23 single-sex physical education classes, and participation in the survey was voluntary. Four surveys from the girls were not completed, and surveys from 101 male respondents were eliminated because they were not completed. The students ranged in age from 13 to 18. The final sample contained 635 students: 330 boys (52%) and 301 girls (48%), 76% of whom had been involved in a dating relationship. The racial distribution included 9.4% Latino, 49.6% Caucasian, 29.8% African American, and 7.3% Asian (remainder were unidentified).

The survey addressed the experience of dating violence in current or past relationships, physical effects of the worst incident of violence, reaction to the worst incident of violence, who initiated the incident, who was told, where the incident occurred, and who was present.

Forty-one percent of the boys and 35% of the girls reported experiencing some form of physical aggression from their partners in any dating relationship. Overall, girls experienced significantly higher levels of severe violence and reported more severe physical and emotional reactions to the violence. Girls were more likely to experience severe violence (which the authors defined as having an object thrown at the victim, being punched, choked, or threatened with a weapon) whereas boys were more likely than girls to experience less severe forms of physical dating violence (defined by the authors as having one's hair pulled or being kicked, scratched, slapped, or pinched).

The extent to which girls used violence for self-defense was revealed when the respondents answered the question about who began the abuse:

> Girls reported their dating partners were the ones who started the abuse 70% of the time, whereas boys reported their dating partners to be the initiators of abuse only 27% of the time. The boys were much more likely to state that incidents were initiated by them. (Molidor & Tolman, 1998, p. 187)

Thirty-seven percent of the girls reported self-defense as the reason they used violence, whereas only 6% of the boys reported self-defense as being the reason for their expressed violent behavior.

Furthermore, this study revealed that a large number of sexually violent episodes took place in schools or on school grounds. Forty-six percent of the students reported that their worst incident of sexual/dating violence occurred on school grounds or in the building. Moreover, 60% of the girls and 51% of the boys stated that they were alone at the time, meaning that 40% of the time for the girls and 49% of the time for the boys, others were present. No significant gender differences were found in where the incident occurred or who was present.

Limitations of the study include use of a convenience sample that prevents the results from being generalized to other locations and populations and a lack of information on students with disabilities or gay/lesbian students.

Jasinski & West (1997)

Although the study by Jasinski and West (1997) did not survey students about the sexual violence in their relationships, it did survey 143 teachers (52 men and 91 women) who worked with students in two New England high schools. They were surveyed in several areas: (a) their ability to judge violent relationships, (b) situational responses to instances of potential and actual violence by giving the teachers four scenarios and asking them to indicate how they would act, (c) rating of dating violence in their school, and (d) their own experiences with personal victimization.

The problem of dating violence was perceived differently by male teachers than by female teachers:

> None of the male teachers thought that there was a serious dating violence problem in their school, whereas 7.5% of the female teachers thought there was a very serious problem. Almost twice as many of the female teachers (21.3%) compared to male teachers (13%) viewed the dating violence problem in their schools as moderately serious . . . compared to male teachers, female teachers are likely to know twice as many students involved in physically abusive relationships. (p. 7)

When the teachers were asked about their actions if they were to witness violent or potentially violent hypothetical situations in their schools, both male and female teachers responded in a similar manner for those scenarios that involved yelling (scenario 1) or sexual name-calling (scenario 2). Both male and female teachers responded that they would first speak to the students, before they took any other actions. However, in scenario 3, which depicts a male student who has yelled at and hit his girlfriend, gender differences in the responses of the teachers emerged:

> Slightly over half of the female teachers compared to almost three-quarters of the male teachers would speak to the student first. More than twice as many female teachers as male teachers would call security first when faced with this type of situation. (p. 8)

Again, in a fourth and final scenario, where the female student indicates that she is afraid to leave the building because of what she fears her boyfriend will do, gender differences between male and female teachers remain in three out of the four choices mentioned by the teachers. For the choices, the survey results were (a) speak to the student (13.7% of male teachers, 6.6% of female teachers); (b) alert security (17.6% of male teachers, 30.8% of female teachers); (c) contact a counselor (21.6% of male teachers, 13.2% of female teachers); and (d) refer to assistant principal (43.1% of male teachers, and 42.9% of female teachers). Finally, previous victimization status, as voluntarily revealed by the respondents, may have had some bearing upon some of the women teachers' reactions, in scenarios 3 and 4 where hitting was involved and where the female student indicated that she was afraid to leave the building.

When the teachers were asked if they had been trained to deal with and prevent dating violence, 11.9% of the women teachers had received some form of training compared to 2% of the men teachers. When asked if they would like to receive training, more than twice as many female teachers than male teachers expressed interest (25.8% of the women compared to 11.5% of the men). However, these numbers still represent a small portion of the total. The teachers' lack of training was manifested in their inability to recognize abusive relationships and their limited repertoire of responses to these potentially violent situations when they did recognize them.

In conclusion, the authors' findings show that even though "a majority of teachers felt capable of identifying an abusive relationship, in fact many were unable to do so. In addition, there was a false sense of security with respect to the incidence of dating violence within their schools" (p. 9).

Since there are very few studies about sexual violence in schools, it is difficult to substantiate firmly the presence of sexual violence in schools. However, combining a few strong studies with the daunting abundance of studies on sexual harassment which offer substantial evidence about sexually violent behaviors that take place in schools, I believe that we can claim with moderate substantiation that sexual violence exists in the nation's schools.

CRIME VICTIMIZATION SURVEYS

Another source of information about sexual violence in schools is the standard crime victimization surveys, largely collected by the Department of Justice, the Centers for Disease Control and Prevention, the Department of Education, and by some private, professionally based organizations. It is to those surveys that we now turn our attention in the hopes of gleaning information as well as determining trends for future research.

The standard sources of survey data on sexual violence in schools are very problematic and contradictory, and in some instances underestimate the occurrences and kinds of sexual violence that take place in schools. Five sources of survey data purportedly about sexual assaults and rapes at schools will be compared to make this point.

National Crime Victimization Survey (1994)

The most comprehensive data is from the 1994 National Crime Victimization Survey (NCVS) conducted by the Bureau of Justice Statistics (BJS) of the Department of Justice, and published in 1997 (BJS, 1997). This survey instrument asked about the location of various crimes, among them sexual assaults and rapes, and the relationship between the target and the perpetrator of the crimes.

In 1994, according to data from the NCVS, there were an estimated 152,690 incidents of rape or sexual assault throughout the United States that were perpetrated by people who were strangers to the victim. Of this total, 3.6% (5,497 incidents) of the attacks occurred inside a school building or on school property. An estimated 273,330 additional incidents of rape or sexual assault were perpetrated by persons who were known by the victim. Of these, 2.4% (6,560 attacks) occurred inside a school building or on school property. These projections were based on fewer than 20 telephone interviews in which people answered yes to NCVS interviewers (Bureau of Justice Statistics, 1997).

The NCVS almost certainly underestimates the actual number of rapes and sexual assaults, however. Most of the survey data are gathered during telephone interviews. Crime victims, and especially rape victims, may be unwilling to admit during a telephone conversation with a survey interviewer that they had been assaulted. Some sex crime victims may not report the crimes because they were attacked by family members, who may be present in the household during the interview. Other victims may not report crimes simply because they do not want family members to overhear. The use of the word *crime* in the title of the survey and other factors may also contribute to under-reporting (Mahoney, 1997). Some of these problems were mitigated, but not eliminated, when the NCVS was redesigned in 1992.

National Adolescent Student Health Survey (1989)

The National Adolescent Student Health Survey (American School Health Association et al., 1989) also reports on victimization at school (see Table 7.1). The report offered details of life in school: 34% of the students reported that someone threatened to hurt them; 14% reported being robbed; and 13% reported being attacked. Missing from the report is a gendered picture of which genders are doing the threatening and attacking to which genders; it may very well be the case that the students were thinking of typical fist fights when they answered this question, and not sexual assaults.

Table 7.1. Prevalence and Frequency of Fighting and at-School Victimization During One Year

	Total	Sex		Grade		Grade 8		Grade 10	
		Male	Female	8th	10th	Male	Female	Male	Female
Students surveyed	11,419	5,682	5,737	5,859	5,560	2,887	2,972	2,795	2,765
Percentage threatened but not hurt at school									
0 times	65.7	61.7	70.1	62.3	68.8	55.4	69.4	66.9	70.8
1 time	17.8	19.1	16.5	19.0	16.8	21.5	16.3	16.9	16.7
2 times	5.6	6.1	5.1	5.5	5.6	6.4	4.7	5.8	5.4
3+ times	10.9	13.4	8.3	13.2	8.8	16.7	9.6	10.4	7.1
Percentage attacked at school									
0 times	87.0	83.3	91.0	83.6	90.2	77.5	90.0	88.6	91.9
1 time	8.0	9.6	6.2	9.5	6.6	12.3	6.6	7.2	5.9
2 times	2.5	3.7	1.2	3.9	1.2	5.7	2.0	1.9	0.4
3+ times	2.5	3.4	1.6	3.0	2.1	4.5	1.4	2.3	1.8
Percentage raped or subjected to an attempted rape at school									
0 times	95.3	96.2	94.4	94.6	96.0	95.0	94.1	97.2	94.6
1 time	2.0	1.3	2.7	2.4	1.7	1.8	2.9	0.8	2.6
2 times	0.6	0.5	0.6	0.5	0.6	0.6	0.5	0.5	0.8
3+ times	2.1	2.0	2.2	2.5	1.8	2.6	2.5	1.5	2.0

Source: National Adolescent Student Health Survey, 1989, p. 62.

National Household Education Survey (NHES:93, 1993)

We enter the realm of vagueness and the land of missed opportunities when we look at data supplied by the National Center for Education Statistics (NCES), of the U.S. Department of Education (Nolin, Davies, & Chandler 1995). According to their report, 2.7 million violent crimes take place annually at or near schools (citing unpublished 1994 NCVS data). In addition, bullying had been added to the list of incidents in NHES:93 along with any kind of physical attack as well as robbery. Unfortunately, the survey did not distinguish sexual assaults or rapes from the broader category of physical attacks, thereby affording very little insight on the nature and extent of sexual violence in schools.

1997 Massachusetts Youth Risk Behavior Survey

Questions about dating violence were added to this survey, which was administered to 3,982 students in Grades 9–12, representing an overall response rate of 70%. In total, 58 out of 66 randomly selected high schools participated in the survey, resulting in a school response rate of 88%. Because of the high response rate, data from the 1997 Massachusetts YRBS have been weighted by the Centers for Disease Control and Prevention (CDC), allowing the information derived from the report to be an accurate estimate of the prevalence of the health-risk behaviors of Massachusetts youth as a whole and of students of both genders and all four high school grades. The racial/ethnic breakdown was 74% White; 6.2% Black; 7.8% Hispanic; 5.5% Asian or Pacific Islander; and 5.4% other (including American Indian and Alaskan Native). Massachusetts was one of 33 states that participated in 1997 in the YRBS.

Dating violence was experienced by 14% of the high school survey participants (7% of the males, 20% of the females). More than 1 in 10 students (11%) had been hurt physically by someone they were dating, and 7% had been hurt sexually. All gender differences were statistically significant, $p < .05$. (Massachusetts Department of Education, 1998.)

Violence and Discipline Problems in U.S. Public Schools (1996–97)

In late March 1998, the U.S. Department of Education released a study based on a nationally representative sample of 1,234 public elementary, middle, and high schools (U.S. Department of Education, 1998). The principals of those schools were asked about crimes, including sexual battery and rape, about which they had contacted the police or law enforcement officials. Based on the survey results, Table 7.2 reveals that approximately 4,170 incidents of rape or sexual battery were reported by U.S. public schools, a figure considerably

Table 7. 2. Number and Percent of Public Schools Reporting Incidents of Rape or Other Type of Sexual Battery*, and Total Number of Incidents of Rape or Other Type of Sexual Battery Reported in Public Schools in Which Police or Other Law Enforcement Were Contacted, by School Characteristics, 1996-1997**

	Number of schools with one or more incidents	Percent of schools with one or more incidents	Total number of incidents
All public schools	2,326	3%	4,170
Instructional level			
Elementary school	404	1%	690
Middle school	731	5%	1,400
High school	1,191	8%	2,070
Size of enrollment			
Less than 300	255	1%	320
300–999	1,232	2%	2,010
1,000 or more	840	11%	1,830
Locale			
City	912	5%	1,930
Urban fringe	708	4%	1,130
Town	256	1%	290
Rural	451	2%	820
Region			
Northeast	333	2%	510
Southeast	595	4%	1,210
Central	661	3%	1,180
West	738	3%	1,270

Source: U.S. Department of Education, National Center for Education Statistics, 1998, pp. 39-40, citing data from a 1997 publication.
* Other types of sexual battery include fondling, indecent liberties, child molestation, and sodomy.
** National projections are based on data from a representative sample of 1,234 public schools.

less than the estimated 12,057 rapes and sexual assaults at school projected by NCVS (Bureau of Justice Statistics, 1997).

Violence by Intimates (1998)

In March 1998, the Bureau of Justice Statistics published a statistical factbook using data from 1992–1996 gathered from sources including the NCVS, Uniform Crime Reporting Program (UCR), and National Incident-Based Reporting System (NIBRS) (Greenfeld et al., 1998). Each year from 1992 through 1996 there were an average of more than 960,000 incidents of violent victimization of girls and women age 12 or older by an intimate. Intimates include former or current spouses, boyfriends, or girlfriends (Greenfeld et al., 1998). Over the 5 years from 1992–1996, 72.2% of the incidents of nonlethal intimate violence against girls and women occurred at or near the victim's home, whereas only 1.2% occurred at schools. That 1.2% of incidents comprises roughly 58,000 nonlethal incidents of intimate violence against girls and young women at school over 5 years. It is likely that the percentage of incidents at school or on school grounds would have been higher if the survey were restricted to girls between the ages of 12–18 years.[1]

All in all, these standard sources of crime data have many limitations, including the language used in the questions they ask, the questions that are not included, and the methods by which they obtain their results. It goes without saying that a full and true portrait of the extent of sexual violence in schools is missing if we only look at standard crime surveys. In the face of such deficiencies and omissions, it becomes important to find alternative, unpublished and nonstandard sources of survey data.

ALTERNATIVE SOURCES OF INFORMATION ON SEXUAL VIOLENCE IN THE SCHOOLS

An alternative way to measure the scope of the problem of teenage sexual violence is to look at the data gathered by sexual assault and domestic violence organizations that work in K–12 schools. A large combined domestic violence and sexual assault organization in Austin, Texas, called SafePlace (formerly called the Center for Battered Women), well known for its dating-violence intervention program and curriculum, *Expect Respect*, agreed to reveal some of their statistics and to share some of the lessons that they have learned through many years of working in schools. Moreover, they had recently been awarded, in collaboration with the Austin (Texas) Independent School District, a grant from the Centers for Disease Control and Prevention (CDC) to conduct a 3-year study of fifth graders connecting interventions to curb bullying with sexual harassment, teen dating violence, and domestic violence.

What they have learned from working in the schools on the problem of violence in teenage relationships has not been published in the usual places, and therefore, the lessons they have derived may only reside among those who work in similar organizations ("member's knowledge" in the language of enthnographers). After years of conducting weekly support groups for both male and female adolescents in both middle and high schools, the project coordinator (who is also the principal investigator in the CDC project mentioned above) reported in a telephone interview that teen dating violence regularly and systematically manifests itself in schools (B. Rosenbluth, personal communication, February 11, 1998). The education director's recommendations for collecting more accurate information include finding alternative words for "dating" when probing adolescents' relationships, and questioning the students (harasser and target) about their relationship when behaviors that adults might characterize as sexual harassment occurs in schools. In other words, what we might really be seeing is a manifestation of dating violence, and not only sexual harassment.

In the 1997-98 school year, this program served 279 teens, including 171 girls and 102 boys (the sex of 6 additional participants was not recorded during a personal interview with a counselor before the groups were formed). Of the 279 teens, 12% reported they had experienced abuse in a current dating/intimate relationship, 39% reported experiencing abuse in a past dating/intimate relationship, and 60% had witnessed/experienced domestic violence (Rosenbluth, personal communication, September 10, 1998). (The data are not necessarily school specific.) All participants agreed to remain in the groups, though some were perhaps referred by school staff whereas others self-referred.

SafePlace also conducts classroom sessions on dating violence. During the 1997-98 school year, 6,124 students participated in these sessions. Data were collected on the dating violence experiences of each classroom participant. One in six (15%) of classroom participants reported that they had been abused in a dating relationship, 10% reported that they had abused a person they were dating, 30% reported that a friend of theirs was abused by someone they were dating, and 19% had a friend who had abused a partner (Rosenbluth, personal communication, September 10, 1998).

In conclusion, by utilizing alternative sources of information, which are often not published in the standard journals and instead reside in the yearly reports of domestic violence and sexual assault agencies such as SafePlace, we might be able to obtain a more accurate accounting of school-based sexual violence, as opposed to relying on the standard crime surveys that seem to underestimate or distort the true picture of sexual violence in schools for girls and young women.

Conclusion

THIS JOURNEY has produced recommendations that might reduce both sexual harassment and sexual violence in schools by creating new public policy, fostering collaboration between social service and community-based organizations and schools, and offering new directions for research. The following recommendations are divided into those that are school based and those that are policy and research based.

SCHOOL-BASED RECOMMENDATIONS

1. Heighten awareness of all school staff (teachers, administrators, cafeteria workers, custodians, bus drivers, coaches, secretaries, and so forth) about sexual harassment and sexual violence, including dating violence, in schools. Establish mandatory professional development training on the subject that is not, for example, an hour's lecture on an early-release day when the staff are herded into the auditorium or cafeteria to listen to a speaker from an outside organization or worse yet, the school board's attorney. Instead, at a minimum, a half-day to full-day interactive training session should be required of all school personnel, with additional training offered to specialized teams made up of both men and women within each school building. These teams would then serve as ombuds (a title that, although perhaps difficult for students to pronounce, is preferable to either "complaint manager" or "grievance coordinator," which are terms guaranteed to turn off the students) to whom students wishing to make complaints would be directed. These teachers/ombuds would also be asked

109

__ include discussions of sexual harassment and sexual violence in their classrooms as part of the regular school curriculum.

2. Foster collaboration between K-12 schools and domestic violence or sexual assault organizations or both. Invite members of those organizations into the classroom for sustained periods of time, working with cross-disciplinary teams of teachers (Stein & Cappello, 1999). School staff should meet with these individuals in advance to review their handouts and lessons and to offer guidance about classroom procedures and expectations. After the series of presentations have concluded, school personnel should offer feedback and recommendations to the agency staff.

3. Create a school-based version of a stay-away or temporary restraining order. This process could be simple, noncontestable by the other party, and enforced by school personnel, with reprisals for violations; it could be as simple as "You stay away from her or else. . . ." Since it is not at all certain how many adolescents would avail themselves of civil orders of protection/temporary restraining orders (discussed below), by creating and offering a school-based version, the process would be simplified and demystified for them. In addition, parental permission might be required, along with oversight from school personnel (all of whom would first have to be informed).

POLICY AND RESEARCH-BASED RECOMMENDATIONS

1. Redesign and readminister sexual harassment surveys. Future surveys should include questions that ask about the relationship between the harasser or perpetrator and the target. Granted that some sexual harassment is conducted in a somewhat anonymous fashion (graffiti, notes, catcalls, and the like), much of it is also identifiable, takes place between people who know each other, and occurs in public. Questions should be added to the sexual harassment surveys that probe for manifestations of dating violence; or the desire of one of the individuals to date the other, who prefers to either terminate the relationship or not to begin it in the first place. Use teenagers as consultants in the development of these survey instruments and pretest with a cohort of teens.

2. Expand eligibility for temporary restraining orders (TROs; also known as orders of protection) to include noncohabiting minors. Unfortunately, the great majority of adolescents in abusive relationships cannot get protections because they are merely dating (as opposed to being married or living together) or do not meet age requirements or some residency requirement (Levesque, 1997). As pointed out in Chapter 6, currently, only 13 states allow for the these protections for minors (with distinctions in

some states made between dating, courtship, and engagement): Alabama, Alaska, California, Colorado, Illinois, Massachusetts, Minnesota, New Hampshire, New Mexico, North Dakota, Oklahoma, Pennsylvania, and West Virginia. These 13 states allow for the most protections offered to adolescents because they do not impose conditions or restrictions, such as parenthood, marriage, cohabitation, or other adult requirements. Three additional states offer protection to adolescents who are 16 years old or older: New York, Utah, and Washington. All of the remaining states limit TRO protection either by excluding minors altogether,[1] requiring the involved minors to be parents together,[2] or requiring them to be or have been married or cohabitants.[3] Only four states expressly allow minors to be the subject of a civil action (meaning that if one's batterer or abuser is a minor, then a TRO could be issued against that person).[4] Five other states require that the subject of the TRO be at least 16 years old.[5] Eight states expressly prohibit minors from being subject to TROs, and the remaining 33 states are silent on the issue.[6] Sadly, such restrictions imply that violence or abuse from a minor is somehow less or different than violence and abuse from someone who is no longer a minor. To quote from Levesque (1997): "The failure to incorporate adolescents into domestic violence policies engenders a brutal social reality: adolescents are left without legal recourse and without mandated or otherwise available services. In essence, therefore, adolescent battering remains invisible" (p. 357). Adolescents will remain in peril until all states offer them eligibility for protection from (sexual) violence from a dating or courting partner.

3. Permit domestic violence and sexual assault organizations to apply for funding under various government programs that would enhance their collaboration with and entry into schools.

4. Add gender-based and gender-motivated crimes to the national and state definitions of hate crimes (such a provision was introduced as a bill to Congress in 1998; and in many states these provisions already carry the force of law). Forty states have hate crimes legislation of some kind; nine states have no hates crimes legislation. Of those states that specify which groups are covered by their hate crimes legislation, only 11 states mention gender (Lyman, 1998).

5. Develop unified definition of sexual violence for federal agencies and surveys.

FINAL THOUGHTS AND HOPES

Beyond the school-based and policy and research-based recommendations listed above, which would be best implemented in a comprehensive, simultaneous approach, I remain hopeful about efforts by classroom teachers to normalize the conversation about sexual harassment and other forms of gender violence in the classroom—to create classroom discussions, with age-appropriate and sequential materials, to the curriculum. Rather than offering reprimands administered in the principal's office or schoolwide assemblies where students are read the riot act and given a pat list of don'ts and do's, and in some cases imposing draconian prohibitions against hand-holding and other forms of mutual affectionate gestures in school (Maroney, 1995), we need to move discussions of sexual harassment from the margins to the mainstream—into the classroom.

Prior to initiating those classroom conversations, educators need to recognize sexual harassment in schools as a form of gendered violence, often performed in public, sometimes in front of adults whose legal responsibility is to provide equal protection and equal educational opportunity. Sexual harassment can be the touchstone for opening the conversation about gendered violence.

Ultimately, a strategy to eliminate and prevent sexual harassment in schools needs to aim at a transformation of the broader school culture. Dealing effectively with sexual harassment is much easier if a school has committed itself to infuse a spirit of equity and a critique of injustice into its curriculum and pedagogy. On the other hand, harassment flourishes where children learn the art of doing nothing in the face of unjust treatment by others. When teachers subject children to an authoritarian pedagogy, they don't learn to think of themselves as moral subjects, capable of speaking out when they witness bullying or other forms of harassment. If students haven't been encouraged to critique the sexism of the curriculum, hidden and overt, then they are less likely to recognize it when they confront it in their midst. Too often, the entire school structure offers children no meaningful involvement in decision making about school policy, climate, or other curriculum matters. Children rehearse being social spectators in their school lives (Bigelow, 1991; Stein, 1993a, 1995a).

We can make a difference in the classroom and beyond when we take up the subjects of bullying, hazing, sexual harassment, and dating violence. When we frame the issue of sexual harassment as one of injustice and civil rights and see the problem from the vantage points of the targets, the harassers, and the observers, we can teach empathy as we also teach children to emphasize and employ intervention strategies (Stein & Cappello, 1999). In this way we see all players as "justice makers" as opposed to social spectators (hooks, 1989, p. 9).

I end this book in the same way that I began, with the words of children. This time, however, with the words of eighth-grade boys who in 1993 were part of a pilot curriculum development project and kept ethnographic journals detailing their observations of sexual harassment in their schools (Stein,

1995a; Stein & Sjostrom, 1994). Their words confirm the experiences of the girls cited at the beginning of and throughout this book—that sexual harassment is present and very public in schools. Even for the boys who are observers, sexual harassment is sometimes scary, troubling, and certainly disruptive to the educational environment.

> Today, as usual, I observed sexist behavior in my art class. Boys taunting girls and girls taunting boys has become a real problem. I wish they would all stop yelling at each other so that for once I could have art class in peace. This is my daily list of words I heard today in art that could be taken as sexual harassment: bitch, hooker, pimp, whore.

> Today for the first time I was witness to sexual harassment in my gym class. A couple of girls came into the exercise room today and suddenly, almost like a reflex, some of the boys began to whistle at them and taunt them. I was surprised since I had never seen this kind of behavior from my gym class before. Some of the boys that I considered my friends even began to do it. It felt awful to watch, but if I said anything it would not stop them and would only hurt me.

> Today in class people reported their findings as ethnographers; that is, they told the class about the examples of sexual harassment they had witnessed. There were some pretty bad examples. It's amazing that this stuff goes on at our school. I think that part of the problem is that some kids don't know what sexual harassment is, so they don't know when they are doing it. One of the things that scared me was that no one said they had any trouble finding examples. Everybody had found at least one or two examples, and most people found many more. I found out that it happens everywhere: in the halls, the cafeteria, or even at basketball try-outs. It happens everywhere that teachers are not in direct supervision of students.

> I think it's good that the eight graders are doing the curriculum at the same time, because then we can discuss it during lunch and stuff. I really do think that people are learning a lot from it. I mean, the person at our table at lunch who used to really be a sexual harasser has stopped and actually turned nice when all the girls at our table told him to stop or we would get Mr. [teacher] into it. I don't think he realized that what he was doing was really making us uncomfortable.

> The sexual harassment [curriculum] is really doing the school some good. One of the harassers who has been always harassing any girl at all has stopped. [X has] stopped goosing and touching girls. I never thought I'd see the day—he no longer pinches girls and rubs up against them in the hall. Now I feel a lot more comfortable in art class. I have art with him, and now I don't have to always, literally, watch my back. And [O] has seen a lot of improvement. People are more conscious about what they say, and how they use words like gay, fag-

got, and lesbian. They realize that some people could really be offended by it. (Stein, 1995a, p. 160)

These journal entries offer hope in the way that they point out the impact that age-appropriate, deliberate, and teacher-led conversations and curriculum can have in the lives of students (Stein, 1995a; Stein & Sjostrom, 1994). By creating a common classroom vocabulary and offering nonpunitive and nonlitigious ways in which to probe controversial and troubling subjects, educators and their students can confront and reduce sexual harassment and gendered violence in the schools. The first step is to recognize that sexual harassment is a common feature in children's school lives and that the students—both the boys and the girls—recognize that most adults are sitting back, watching it happen. The next step is for the adults to name it as the students see it, and to take it on—publicly, in the classroom and throughout the whole school community.

Epilogue

SUPREME COURT RULES IN *DAVIS* CASE THAT SCHOOLS ARE RESPONSIBLE FOR STUDENT-TO-STUDENT SEXUAL HARASSMENT

On May 24, 1999, in a 5-to-4 decision, the U.S. Supreme Court ruled that schools are indeed liable for student-to-student sexual harassment, if they knew about the harassment and had failed to stop it. Justice Sandra Day O'Connor, writing for the majority in *Davis v. Monroe County Board of Education* (119 S.Ct. 1661), indicated that school districts would be liable under federal law Title IX "only if they were 'deliberately indifferent' to information about 'severe, pervasive, and objectively' offensive harassment among students" (Walsh, 1999, p. 22). Joined in the majority opinion by Justices John Paul Stevens, David H. Souter, Ruth Bader Ginsburg, and Stephen G. Breyer, this decision now sends the six-year legal battle back to the district court level for trial, reversing the decision of the U.S. Court of Appeals for the Eleventh Circuit.

The reaction of the dissenting Justices seemed more bitter than those of the attorneys who lost the case. Julie Underwood, the general counsel for the National School Board Association, who served as co-counsel for the defendant, the Monroe County School Board, called the decision "a standard we can live with and in fact are living up to already" (Greenhouse, 1999, p. A24). "It gives school districts some flexibility, so they won't be litigating over every student peck on the cheek of another student" (Walsh, 1999, p. 1).

On the other hand, the blistering dissent, half again as long as the majority opinion at 34 pages, written by Justice Anthony M. Kennedy, was delivered from the bench in an unusual departure from the Court's customary practice. The dissent, signed by Justices Kennedy, Antonin Scalia, and Clarence

Thomas, along with Chief Justice William H. Rehnquist, warned of federal intrusion into "day-to-day classroom logistics and interactions" and overreaction to behaviors that were characterized as "routine problems of adolescence" (Greenhouse, 1999, p. A24).

While Justice Kennedy may have characterized this case as teaching "little Johnny a perverse lesson in Federalism," Justice O'Connor rejoined by saying that it "assures that little Mary may attend class" (Greenhouse, 1999, p. A1).

Additional Sexual Harassment Surveys

STATE SPECIFIC SURVEYS

Massachusetts (1980–1981)

One of the earliest surveys on the issue of sexual harassment in K-12 schools was conducted in the 1980-81 school year by the Massachusetts Department of Education (Stein, 1981, 1982). Of the 49 boys and girls who filled out surveys, 38 reported incidences of sexual harassment, 16 of which were peer to peer (all but one directed at a girl by a boy or group of boys); the remaining 22 incidences were episodes in which adults in the school community reportedly harassed students.

The second component of the Massachusetts Department of Education's investigation into sexual harassment was composed of interviews with young women who had entered shops and courses in vocational schools that had previously been considered as nontraditional for their sex. Out of 22 such young women interviewed, 19 had experienced at least one incident of sexual harassment.

The chief limitation of the Massachusetts study is its reliance on a rather small convenience sample. It is, nonetheless, recognized as groundbreaking in light of its historical period and context. At the time of the study, there were no sexual harassment lawsuits in the K-12 arena. There was only one legal precedent in higher education—the case against Yale University, in which it was ruled that sexual harassment was a form of sex discrimination (*Alexander v. Yale University*, 1977, 1980).

Iowa (1994)

The 1994 Iowa survey had a sample of 503 students (253 females, 250 males) and found 83% of the female students and 62% of the male students reported at least one "exposure" to sexually harassing situations (*exposure* was defined as an experience with sexual harassment). Out of 400 high schools in Iowa, 83 principals agreed to participate in the study (21% response rate), with parental permission/opt-out available: Surveys were administered in physical education classes, in addition to telephone interviews with students at their homes.

Comparing the findings of this study to others is made difficult because of the authors' use of the awkward concept of "exposure" to sexual harassment rather than the simpler, cleaner notion of "experience." Use of this term could have added some confusion for the students taking the survey and thus decreases comparability with other surveys. Moreover, the authors decided to avoid using the expression *sexual harassment* in the survey and during the interview phase of this study because they found that the term was responsible for "triggering emotional responses" (Boddy & Selzer, 1994, p. 3). Another limitation of the study is that no ethnic/racial information was provided.

North Dakota (1997)

Using a version of the AAUW poll instrument in eight randomly selected high schools of varying student size across the state of North Dakota, 87 males and 89 females in the 12th grade were surveyed in social studies classes. The researchers (Stratton & Backes, 1997) found that males in the North Dakota sample were more likely than males in the nationally representative AAUW poll to report experiencing sexual harassment. In the North Dakota sample 83% of the boys reported experiencing sexual harassment, whereas in the AAUW poll 60% of the boys had experienced sexual harassment. For girls, 93% of the girls in the North Dakota survey reported that they had experienced sexual harassment compared to 83% of the girls in the AAUW poll. The researchers also found that the most frequent types of sexual harassment identified were sexual comments, jokes, gestures, or looks, a finding consistent with results from other surveys. The most frequent type of harassment was student to student, but eight females (9.8%) reported being harassed by a teacher and two females (2.4%) by a coach whereas five boys (6.9%) reported being harassed by a coach and two (2.8%) by a teacher. These percentages are considerably lower than the AAUW study.

Limitations of this study include that it sampled only students in the 12th grade. Comparisons with the AAUW survey should not be made despite the authors' best intentions to replicate that study. Differences in prevalence could be due to the age of the respondents. The study gave no information about class or racial or ethnic diversity, and no mention of disabled or gay/lesbian youth.

Texas (1997)

In October 1997, the Texas Civil Rights Project released its study of peer-to-peer sexual harassment in schools (Texas Civil Rights Project, 1997). The study was based on data from 1,860 students in Grades 7–12 who were participating in workshops on sexual harassment. The sample included 784 males, 886 females, and 190 others who did not specify their sex. Students did not self-select for the training—they were assigned because participation was required. In some schools, permission slips were required from parents.

Notwithstanding the limitations posed by the use of a convenience sample, the results mirrored some of the findings from the AAUW poll (1993) and the *Seventeen* magazine study (Stein, Marshall, & Tropp, 1993; "Sexual Harassment is Rampant," 1997). The Texas study found that 64% of the female students had experienced sexual gestures, looks, comments, or jokes. More than half (52%) of the female students reported having been pressured into doing something sexual against their will; and 25% of all students surveyed had experienced unwanted physical invasions such as touching, pinching, and grabbing.

Limitations of this study are many: Surveys were distributed after workshops devoted to the subject of sexual harassment, thus providing a bias in the sampling. The report on the study was written by lawyers with little research experience, making, among other problems, access to the information awkward and difficult to obtain. For example, the authors did not report a breakdown of the sample by sex or grade of the survey respondents.

SCHOOL-BASED STUDIES

Shakeshaft and Doctoral Students (1992–1995)

The research of Charol Shakeshaft at Hofstra University with a team of graduate assistants from 1992–1995 looked at 1,000 middle school/junior high students in eight schools on Long Island, New York (Shakeshaft, 1997). Unlike others whose studies have relied on paper-and-pencil surveys to gather data, this team of researchers gathered data from naturalistic observations and interviews. Students and school administrators from a cross-section of socioeconomic classes, races, and high- and low-achieving school districts were observed in school and interviewed both in and out of school.

A key finding from this study was that girls were more likely to be made fun of because of their appearance, whereas boys were more often teased because of their actions or behavior. Girls tended to be targeted for harassment if they were unattractive or unfashionable, or, on the other hand, if they were more physically mature than their peers and therefore coded as pretty or fast sexually. Boys were targeted if they did not fit the stereotypic masculine mode (Shakeshaft, 1997).

One limitation of this study its use of the term *peer abuse*, the definition of which did not correspond either to the legal definition of "sexual harassment" or "child (sexual) abuse." Moreover, there was no published breakdown of the observations or interviews by gender and no published interview schedule or coding scheme. The research has been presented in very preliminary ways, without much substantiation.

Roscoe, Strouse, & Goodwin (1994)

This study, conducted by Roscoe, Strouse, and Goodwin (1994), surveyed 561 white students (281 females and 280 males) in a midwestern intermediate school. The students ranged in age from 11 to 16 years. Students were asked whether they had experienced peer sexual harassment and about their acceptance of sexually harassing behaviors. The survey consisted of 13 questions and addressed the following specific harassing behaviors: sexual comments, teasing, sexual gossip/rumors, phone calls, pressure for dates, touching, rubbing, pinching, grabbing, pushing, sexual advances, pressure for sexual activity, and sexual assault. Nearly half (43%) of the students reported that they had experienced peer sexual harassment (50% of females and 37% of males). The study also found that both boys and girls found sexual harassment unacceptable.

The results of the study cannot be generalized to other school populations because data were collected from a small convenience sample. In addition, the study collected no information on socioeconomic status, and provided no information on the harassment of disabled or gay/lesbian youth.

Fineran and Bennett (1995)

Begun as a doctoral dissertation project, this study surveyed 342 male and female students in a large, midwestern, urban high school. The grade breakdown was 70 freshmen, 82 sophomores, 82 juniors, and 105 seniors. The school had a high percentage of minority students (43% African American, 24% Latino, 14% White, 11% Asian, and 6% other or unidentified).[1] Students were asked about any sexual harassment that they might have experienced, perpetrated, or witnessed. Other questions asked how upset or threatened they were by any harassment they endured as victim or witness and about the nature of any relationship between themselves and the perpetrator(s). Students also completed two scales measuring beliefs about personal and gender-based power.

The study found that 84% of the students had experienced peer sexual harassment (87% of the females and 79% of the males). Three fourths (75%) of the students reported perpetrating sexual harassment. The boys were twice as likely as the girls to report perpetrating sexual harassment. More than half (60%) of the harassing incidents were perpetrated by a schoolmate whom the target knew casually, 25% were perpetrated by students in dating or ex-dating relationships, and 15% were perpetrated by a schoolmate whom the target did not know (Fineran & Bennett, 1995).

The results of this study cannot be generalized to other high school populations because it surveyed a convenience sample of students. The study also provides no information on disabled or gay/lesbian youth.

New Jersey (1995)

Using the AAUW instrument, this study surveyed all 711 students (46% female and 54% male) in a single New Jersey high school ("Sexual Harassment in a New Jersey High School: A Replication Study," 1995). The students were divided among Grades 9 (25%), 10 (34%), and 11 (32%) (the report does not indicate the grade of the remaining 9%). The self-reported racial breakdown of the students was as follows: White/Caucasian (64%), African American (10%), Asian (10%), other (10%), and unidentified (6%).

Three fourths (76%) of the students believed that sexual harassment happened in their school, and 73% had personally experienced it. Most of the reported episodes of harassment occurred in public places, 47% in the hallways and 29% in the classroom. The results from this one school in New Jersey were in general agreement with the original AAUW study, although the reported levels of sexual harassment were slightly lower in the New Jersey school than they were in the national sample.

The study relied upon a convenience sample, so its findings cannot be generalized to other high schools. In addition, the study provides no information about the socioeconomic status of the students or the harassment of disabled or gay/lesbian youth.

Notes

INTRODUCTION

1. Federal Title IX of the Education Amendments of 1972, 20 U.S.C. § 1681 (P.L. 92-318, states): "No person in the United States shall, on the basis of sex, be excluded from participation in, be denied the benefits of, or be subjected to discrimination under any education program or activity receiving federal financial assistance."

2. *Boys Will Be Boys*, ABC after-school special, produced by Little Eagle Productions, first aired on September 15, 1994, and rebroadcast several times, was based on the complaint in Duluth, Minnesota, filed by Katy Lyle. CBS aired an after-school special called *Sexual Considerations* on October 20, 1992. *She Stood Alone*, which aired in the winter of 1995–1996 was loosely based on the sexual harassment complaint of Heather Wright in Mason City, Iowa. In November 1996, another made-for-television movie tackled the subject of a high school girl having an affair with a popular teacher and coach—this show was based on the *Doe v. Taylor* case. A month later (December 16, 1996), yet another made-for-television movie, *Stand Against Fear*, aired on NBC, portraying a high school girl who confronted two football players who had harassed her and the other teammates. This show was loosely based on a lawsuit, *Krengel v. Santa Clara (CA) Unified School District*, which ultimately was settled out of court on June 12, 1997, in favor of the girls. This lawsuit, known as the "Teddie Bears" suit, involved a group of girls who resigned en masse from their support squad rather than endure the harassment from the athletes, whose behaviors were overlooked and disregarded by their coaches and principal (see Chapter 2 for a larger discussion of these lawsuits).

3. See, e.g., Adler (1992); Atkins (1992); Bernstein (1997); Colino (1993a&b); Coolidge (1996); Gross (1992); Ingrassia (1993); Kutner (1994); Lanpher (1992); LeBlanc (1992, 1993); Lewin (1994, 1995); Lyle (1993); Rosen (1993); Rubenstein (1993); Saltzman (1993); Seal (1994); Shannon (1993); Spaid (1993a&b).

4. See, e.g., Bogart & Stein (1987); Brown (1993); Eaton (1993); Higginson (1993); Johnson & Lennon (1997); Lawton (1993, 1994); Lee et al. (1996); Makynen (1998); Mentell (1993); Million (1993); Natale (1993); Pitsch (1995); Shakeshaft (1997); Stein (1991, 1992c, 1993c, 1993d, 1996, 1999); Strauss (1988); Viadero (1997); Webb et al. (1997); Weiss (1994); Yaffe (1995).

CHAPTER 1

1. Wisconsin, Pupil Nondiscrimination Law, Section 118.13, Wis. Statutes, 1985; Administrative Rule PI 9, 1986; Connecticut Discrimination in Public Schools, P.L 97-247, 1997; Rhode Island, Board of Regents policy statement on discrimination based on sexual orientation, 1997.

CHAPTER 2

1. "'Reasonable woman (person) standard.' For both *quid pro quo* and *hostile environment* harassment, whether or not sexual harassment exists is to be judged from the perspective of the 'reasonable person.' That is, would a reasonable person view the behavior complained of as sexual harassment? There is some uncertainty among federal courts and agencies as to whether the 'reasonable person' standard takes into account the circumstances of the victim, and if so, to what extent. Federal agencies such as the EEOC and OCR, as well as several lower courts that have addressed the issue, have adopted a 'reasonable woman' or 'reasonable person in the victim's situation' standard that would appear to favor the complainant more than the 'reasonable person' perspective. . . . Moreover, in several Title IX Letters of Finding, OCR states that the existence of a sexually hostile environment is determined from the viewpoint of a reasonable person in the victim's situation" (Sneed & Woodruff, 1994, p. 10).

2. The Civil Rights Act of 1871, 42 U.S.C. § 1983, states: "Every person who, under color of any statute, ordinance, regulation, custom, usage, of any state or territory, subjects or causes to be subjected, any citizen of the United States or any person within the jurisdiction thereof to the deprivation of any rights, privileges, or immunities secured by the Constitution and laws, shall be liable to the party injured in an action at law, suit in equity, or other proper proceeding for redress."

Section 1983, which is a federal statute, provides an avenue of redress for individuals who have been deprived of their federal constitutional or statutory rights at the behest of the state authority (e.g., the right to due process) and also of federal statutory rights passed pursuant to constitutional authority.

3. Office for Civil Rights' letters of findings or settlement agreements obtained through Freedom of Information Act (FOIA): Millis, Massachusetts (#01-93-1123, issued May 19, 1994); Petaluma, California (#09-89-1050, May 5, 1989); Meridian, Texas (#06-92-1145, July 29, 1992); Washoe County School District, Reno, Nevada (09-91-

1220, March 27, 1993); Sweet Home, Oregon (#10-92-1088, November 15, 1991); Mason City, Iowa (#07-93-1095, March 28, 1994); Albion, Michigan (#15-94-1029, April 7, 1994); Fayetteville, Arkansas (#06-97-1182, June 17, 1998); and Victor Valley Union High School District, Victorville, California (09-90-1143, August 8, 1990).

CHAPTER 3

1. *Davis v. Monroe County (GA) Board of Education*, 1994; *Harms v. Independent School District #47 (Sauk Rapids–Rice)*, 1993; *Eden Prairie School District #272, MN*, 1993; *Modesto City Schools, CA*, 1993; *Newark Unified School District, CA*, 1993 (also see Stein, 1995a).

CHAPTER 4

1. Personal communication with a young woman whose name had appeared on the list 4 years ago.

2. Personal communication with a graduate student who had been visiting the school and had seen the lists.

CHAPTER 7

1. The estimate of 58,000 incidents is based on data from Greenfeld et al., 1998, p. 37. There were 4,819,009 violent victimizations (lethal and nonlethal) of women by intimates from 1992 to 1996. Over the same 5-year period, 7,088 women were murdered by intimates. Subtracting this latter sum from the earlier total number of violent victimizations of women, yields the total number of nonlethal victimizations of women perpetrated by intimates: 4,811,921. Multiplying this figure by 1.2% yields the final estimate: 58,000 incidents.

CONCLUSION

1. Indiana, Iowa, Missouri, New Jersey, and Texas exclude all minors from receiving TRO protection.

2. Arizona, Connecticut, Florida, Georgia, Idaho, Kentucky, Maine, Nebraska, Nevada, North Carolina, South Carolina, South Dakota, Virginia, and Wyoming require minors to be coparents in order to receive TRO protection.

3. Arkansas, Delaware, Hawaii, Kansas, Louisiana, Maryland, Michigan, Mississippi, Montana, Ohio, Oregon, Rhode Island, Tennessee, Vermont, and Wisconsin require minors to be or have been married or cohabitants.

4. Alaska, Idaho, Illinois, and Massachusetts allow all minors to be the subject of civil actions.

5. Connecticut, Oklahoma, Utah, Washington, and Wyoming require that the subject of a TRO be at least 16 years old.

6. Arizona, Colorado, Iowa, Missouri, New Jersey, Oregon, Tennessee, and Wisconsin forbid minors from being subject to TROs.

APPENDIX

1. Reported numbers and percentages do not total 100%.

References

ACLU sues MO school over student's personal web site. (1998, September 4). *School Law News, 26*(18), p. 2.

Adler, J. (1992, October 19). Must boys always be boys? *Newsweek, 120*(16), 77.

Administrators' handling of athlete's "hazing" did not violate Title IX, 10th Circuit says. (1996, June). *Educator's Guide to Controlling Sexual Harassment, 3*(9), 1-3.

Ahmad, Y., & Smith, P. K. (1994). Bullying in schools and the issue of sex differences. In J. Archer (ed.), *Male Violence* (pp. 70-83). New York: Routledge.

Alexander v. Yale University, 459 F. Supp. 1 (D. Conn. 1977); *aff'd on other grounds,* 631 F.2d 178 (2d Cir. 1980).

American Association of University Women (AAUW). (1991). *Shortchanging girls, shortchanging America: A call to action.* Washington, DC: Author.

American Association of University Women (AAUW). (1993). *Hostile hallways: The AAUW survey on sexual harassment in America's schools.* Washington, DC: Author.

American School Health Association, Association for the Advancement of Health Education, & Society for Public Health Education, Inc. (1989). *The national adolescent student health survey: A report on the health of America's youth.* Oakland, CA: Third Party Publishing Co.

Atkins, A. (1992, August). Sexual harassment: Is your child at risk? *Better Homes and Gardens, 70*(8), 32-34.

Bai, M. (1996, July 26). SJC says school wrong to ban T-shirt. *Boston Globe*, pp. B1, 6.

Banks, R. (1997). *Bullying in schools.* ERIC Digest. Champaign, IL: ERIC Clearinghouse on Elementary and Early Childhood Education. (Report No. EDO-PS-97-17, ERIC Document Reproduction Service No. ED 407 154)

Basu, R. (1994a, May 2). Ames girls teach sensitivity lesson, *Des Moines Register*, p. T1.

Basu, R. (1994b, June 9). Girls give a hoot about free speech, *USA Today*, p. 11A.

Benedict, J. (1997). *Public heroes, private felons: Athletes and crimes against women*. Boston: Northeastern University Press.

Bennett, L., & Fineran, S. (1998). Sexual and severe physical violence of high school students: Power beliefs, gender, and relationship. *American Journal of Orthopsychiatry, 64*(4), 645–652.

Bergman, L. (1992, January). Dating violence among high school students. *Social Work, 1*(37), 21–27.

Bernstein, L. (1997, March). Sexual harassment: How to protect your child. *McCalls,* 106–109.

Bethel School District No. 403 v. Fraser, 478 U.S. 675 (1986).

Bigelow, B. (1991). Talking back to Columbus: Teaching for justice and hope. *Rethinking Columbus* (pp. 38–43). Milwaukee: Rethinking Schools.

Boddy, P., & Selzer, J. (1994, March). *Sexual harassment in Iowa high schools: Report of a statewide survey*. Des Moines, IA: Boddy Media Group.

Bogart, K., & Stein, N. (1987). Breaking the silence: Sexual harassment in education. *Peabody Journal of Education, 64*(4), 146–163.

Bowles v. Floresville (TX) Independent School District, No. SA-93-CA-515 (W.D. Tex. 1993, 1994).

Brelis, M. (1993, August 25). Chelmsford students sue over AIDS presentation. *Boston Globe*, pp. 1B, 27.

Brown v. Hot, Sexy and Safer Productions, Inc., 68 F.3d 525 (1st Cir. Oct. 23, 1995).

Brown, A. (1993, October). Sexual harassment by children: Lessons from Eden Prairie. *Here's How, 12*(2), 1–4. Arlington, VA: National Association of Elementary School Principals.

Brown, A. (1994a, February). OCR declines to investigate male student's harassment claim. *Educator's Guide to Controlling Sexual Harassment, 1*(5), 1–2.

Brown, A. (1994b, May). Same-sex harassment by students proves a tough issue for U.S. enforcement agency. *Educator's Guide to Controlling Sexual Harassment, 1*(8), 1–3.

Brown, A. (1995, January). Hazing or sexual harassment? Football player appeals ruling. *Educator's Guide to Controlling Sexual Harassment, 2*(4), 5.

Bruneau v. South Kortright (NY) Central School District, 935 F. Supp. 162 (N.D.N.Y. 1996), *aff'd*, 163 F.3d 749 (2d Cir. 1998).

Bureau of Justice Statistics (1997, May). Criminal victimization in the United States (A national crime victimization survey report, NCJ-162126). Washington, DC: Author.

Burns, D. (1994, April 20). Four students suspended over T-shirt controversy, *Ames Daily Tribune*, pp. A1–2.

Burrow v. Postville (IA) Community School District, F. Supp. 1193 (N.D. Iowa, 1996).

Cal. Ed. Code §§ 212.5 & 212.6 (West Supp. 1994), 48900.2 (West Supp. 1993).

Carlson, M. (1995, January 27). Harassment a problem for many in high school. *Hartford Courant*, pp. 3, 10.

Colino, S. (1993a, February). Are guys' rude comments driving you crazy? *YM, 64.*

Colino, S. (1993b, June/July). Fooling around or sexual harassment? *Parenting, 7*(6), 30.

Coolidge, S. (1996, September 18). In the halls of learning, students get lessons in sexual harassment. *Christian Science Monitor,* pp. 1, 8.

Court absolves schools of student sex harassment (1997, September 5). *School Law News, 25*(18), 1, 3.

Court carves new path in sexual harassment cases. (1997, September 5). *School Law News, 25*(18), 3-4.

Court dismisses male student's Title IX harassment claim. (1994, November 18). *School Law News, 22*(23), 7.

Court rules New Hampshire school district may be liable under Title IX for failing to curtail peer harassment (1997, September). *Educator's Guide to Controlling Sexual Harassment, 4*(12), 1-3.

Davis v. Monroe County (GA) Board of Education, 862 F. Supp. 863 (M.D. Ga. 1994), *rev'd,* 120 F.3d 1390 (11th Cir. 1997) (en banc), *rev'd and remanded to district court,* 119 S.Ct. 1661 (1999).

Davis, W. A. (1996, January 10). When the shirt hits the fan, *Boston Globe,* pp. C25, 28.

Discrimination in public schools, Conn. Gen. Stat. §§ 10-15c, P.L. 91-58, *amended by* P.L. 97-247, § 6 (1997).

Doe v. Antioch (CA) Unified School District, No. C94-01307 [Contra Costa County Super. Ct. (Calif.) October 1, 1996].

Doe v. Lago Vista (TX) Independent School District, 106 F.3d 1223 (5th Cir. 1997).

Jane Doe v. Taylor Independent School District, 15 F.3d 443 (5th Cir. 1994).

Downes, M. (1994, October 29). Student's T-shirt episode wins her a trip to jail. *Boston Herald,* pp. 1, 10.

East Side Union High School District, CA, No. 09-93-1293-I (Office for Civil Rights, U.S. Department of Education, San Francisco, Calif. Nov. 19, 1993).

Easton, N. (1994, October 2). The law of the schoolyard. *Los Angeles Times,* pp. 16-24.

Eaton, S. (1993, July/August). Sexual harassment at an early age: New cases are changing the rules for schools. *Harvard Education Letter, 9*(4), 1-4.

Eden Prairie School District #272, MN, No. 05-92-1174 (Office for Civil Rights, U.S. Department of Education, Chicago, Ill. April 27, 1993).

Eder, D. (1997). Sexual aggression within the school culture. In B. Bank and P. Hall (Eds.), *Gender, equity, and schooling: Policy and practice* (pp. 93-112). New York: Garland.

Eder, D., with Evans, C. C., & Parker, S. (1995). *School talk: Gender and adolescent culture.* New Brunswick, NJ: Rutgers University Press.

Fayetteville School District, AR. No. 06-97-1182, Office for Civil Rights, U.S. Department of Education, Dallas, TX, June 17, 1998.

Fineran, S., & Bennett, L. (1995, July). *Gender and power issues of peer sexual harassment among teenagers.* Paper presented at Fourth International Family Violence Research Conference, University of New Hampshire, Durham, NH.

Fineran, S., & Bennett, L. (1998). Teenage peer sexual harassment: Implications for social work practice in education. *Social Work, 43*(1), 55-64.

Fineran, S., & Bennett, L. (1999). Gender issues of peer sexual harassment among teenagers. *Journal of Interpersonal Violence, 14*(6), 626-641.

Floyd v. Waiters, 113 F.3d 786 (11th Cir. 1998).

Foshee, V. (1996). Gender differences in adolescent dating abuse prevalence. *Health Education Research, 11*(3), 275–286.

Fossey, R., & DeMitchell, T. (1997, March 19). Litigating school dress codes: Are the courts playing trivial pursuit? *Education Week, 16*(25), 42, 47.

Franklin v. Gwinnett County Public Schools, 112 S.Ct. 1028 (1992).

Fuson, K. (1994, August 5). Teens suing 3 schools over harassment. *Des Moines Register*, pp. 1, 3A.

Garcia, I. F., & Perez, G. Q. (1989). Violence, bullying, and counseling in the Iberian Peninsula: Spain. In E. Roland & E. Munthe (Eds.), *Bullying: An international perspective* (pp. 41–52). London: David Fulton.

Gaura, M. (1996, January 5). High school suspends 4 boys for sexual harassment. *San Francisco Chronicle*, p. A19.

Gaura, M. (1997, June 12). Peer harassment suit settled. *San Francisco Chronicle*, p. A19.

Gay, Lesbian, and Straight Education Network. (1997). *Grading our schools: The national report evaluating our nation's schools and their progress on creating safe and affirming learning environments for gay and lesbian students and staff*. New York: Author.

Gebser v. Lago Vista Independent School District, 118 S.Ct. 1206 (1998).

Gladfelter, L. (1994, October 27). White Zombies protest turns into witch hunt for MA high school honor student, Geffen Records (press release).

Good news for schools: Supreme Court limits liability for teacher-student harassment. (1998, August). *Educator's Guide to Controlling Sexual Harassment, 5*(11), 1, 3–5.

Goodman, E. (1996, October 13). The truth behind "the kiss." *Boston Globe*, pp. F1, 8.

Greenberger, M. D., & Williams, V. L. (1998, June 30). Sex harassment and double standards. *New York Times*, p. A23.

Greenfeld, L. A., Rand, M. R., Craven, D., Klaus, P. A., Perkins, C. A., Ringel, C., Warchol, G., Maston, C., & Fox, J. A. (1998). *Violence by intimates: Analysis of data on crimes by current or former spouses, boyfriends, and girlfriends*. NCJ-167237. Washington, DC: Bureau of Justice Statistics, Department of Justice.

Greenhouse, L. (1998, March 8). Court to examine sex harassment. *New York Times*, p. A22.

Greenhouse, L. (1998, June 23). School districts are given a shield in sex harassment. *New York Times*, pp. A1, 14.

Greenhouse, L. (1999, May 25). Sex harassment in class is ruled schools' liability. *New York Times*, pp. A1, A24.

Gross, J. (1992, March 11). Schools are newest arena for sex-harassment cases. *New York Times*, p. B8.

Harms v. Independent School District #47 (Sauk Rapids–Rice), No. ED1990019 (Minnesota Department of Human Rights May 14, 1993).

Hazelwood School District v. Kuhlmeier, 484 U.S. 260 (1988).

Hazing or sexual harassment? Football player appeals rulings. (1995, January). *Educator's Guide to Controlling Sexual Harassment, 2*(4), 5.

Henton, J., Rodney, C., Koval, J., Lloyd, S., & Christopher, S. (1983, September). Romance and violence in dating relationships. *Journal of Family Issues, 4*(3), 476–482.

Higginson, N. M. (1993, November). Addressing sexual harassment in the classroom. *Educational Leadership, 51*(3), 93–96.

Hohler, B. (1992, October 7). Court's shield can draw a bullet. *Boston Globe*, pp. 1, 26.

Hohler, B. (1993, March 23). More college students turn to the courts for protection. *Boston Globe*, pp. 1, 22.

hooks, b. (1989). *Talking back: Thinking feminist, thinking Black*. Boston: South End Press.

Ingrassia, M., Pryor, T., & Friday, C. (1993, December 13). Boy meets girl, boy beats girl. *Newsweek*, 66–68.

Iowa judge overturns jury verdict for victim. (1996, September 20). *School Law News, 24*(19), 3–4.

J. O., P. O. v. Alton Community School District 11, 909 F.2d 267 (7th Cir. 1990).

J. W. v. Bryan Independent School District, 96-1422, *cert. denied*, 519 U.S. 861 (1997).

Jane Doe v. University of Illinois, 138 F.3d 653 (7th Cir. 1998).

Jasinski, J., & West, C. (1997, July). *Not in my school: High school teachers knowledge of and response to dating violence*. Paper presented at the Fifth International Family Violence Conference, Durham, NH.

John B. v. Orland (CA) Joint Union School District (E.D. Calif. 1996).

Johnson, K., & Lennon, S. (1997, Summer). Sexual harassment in schools: Strategies for prevention. *Journal of Family and Consumer Sciences, 89*(2), 20–24.

Jones, M. M. (1994, December 19). Student sues school for sexual harassment by other students. *Lawyer's Weekly USA, 94*(26), 1, 12–13.

Junger, M. (1990). Intergroup bullying and racial harassment in the Netherlands. *Sociology and Social Research, 74*, 65–72.

Keise, C. (1992). *Sugar and spice? Bullying in single-sex schools*. Staffordshire, UK: Trentham Books.

Kowalczyk, L. (1993, July 19–22). A date with danger. *Patriot Ledger* [Quincy, MA], pp. 1–12.

Krengel v. Santa Clara Unified School District, C96 20721 (N.D. Calif. 1997).

Kutner, L. (1994, February 24). Harmless teasing or sexual harassment? *New York Times*, p. C11.

Lagerspetz, K. M., Bjorqkvist, K., Berts, M., & King, E. (1982). Group aggression among school children in three schools. *Scandinavian Journal of Psychology, 23*, 45–52.

Lanpher, K. (1992, May/June). Reading, 'riting, and 'rassment. *Ms*, 90–91.

Lawton, M. (1993, February 10). Sexual harassment of students target of district policies. *Education Week, 12*(20), 1, 15–16.

Lawton, M. (1994, April 27). N.E.A. to publish curriculum on sexual harassment. *Education Week, 13*(31), 5.

Lawton, M. (1996, February 21). District may be held liable for harassment, Court rules. *Education Week, 15*(22), 5.

LeBlanc, A. (1992, September). Harassment in the halls. *Seventeen,* pp. 162–165, 170.

LeBlanc, A. (1993, May). Harassment at school: The truth is out. *Seventeen,* pp. 134–135.

Lee, V. E., Croninger, R. G., Linn, E., & Chen, X. (1996). The culture of sexual harassment in secondary schools. *American Educational Research Journal, 33*(2), 383–417.

Lefkowitz, B. (1997). *Our guys: The Glen Ridge rape and the secret life of the perfect suburb.* Berkeley and Los Angeles, CA: University of California Press.

Levesque, R. (1997). Dating violence, adolescents, and the law. *Virginia Journal of Social Policy & the Law, 4*(2), 339–379.

Levy, B. (1991). *Dating violence: Young women in danger.* Seattle, WA: Seal Press.

Lewin, T. (1994, July 15). Students seeking damages for sex bias. *New York Times,* p. B12.

Lewin, T. (1995, June 26). Students use law on discrimination in sex-abuse suits. *New York Times,* pp. A1, 13.

Lewin, T. (1998, February 7). Schools are moving to police students' off-campus lives. *New York Times,* pp. A1, 23.

Locy, T. (1994, April 14). Dates, families driven to court for protection from violent youths. *Boston Globe,* pp. 25, 33.

Luthro, M. (1994, April 27). Debate staged over hooters, cocks shirts, *Iowa State Daily,* p. 1.

Lydiard, B. W. (1993, January). A decade of dealing with sexual harassment. *School Administrator, 1*(50), 20–21.

Lyle v. Independent School District #709, No. ED341-GSS5-6N (Minnesota Department of Human Rights Sept. 18, 1991).

Lyle, K. (1993, January). Sexual harassment in the boy's room. *Choices, 8*(3), 20–23.

Lyman, R. (1998, October 18). Hate laws don't matter, except when they do. *New York Times,* WK6.

Mahoney, P. (1997, July). *What domestic and sexual violence researchers should know about the redesigned national crime victimization survey.* Paper presented at the Fifth International Family Violence Research Conference, Durham, NH.

Makepeace, J. M. (1981). Courtship violence among college students. *Family Relations, 30,* 97–102.

Makynen, E. (1998, January/February). Teaching about sexual harassment. *What's New in Home Economics, 31*(3), 38.

Malik, S., Sorenson, S. B., & Aneshensel, C. S. (1997). Community and dating violence among adolescents: Perpetration and victimization. *Journal of Adolescent Health, 21*(5), 291–302.

Mass. Gen. Laws Ann., ch. 209A, West 1991).

Massachusetts Anti-discrimination Law, Gen. Law ch. 76, § 5 (amended March 10, 1994).

Massachusetts Department of Education. (1998, April). *1997 Massachusetts youth risk behavior survey results.* Boston: Author.

Mennone v. Gordon, 889 F. Supp. 53 (D. Conn., 1995).

Mentell, E. J. (1993, November). What to do to stop sexual harassment at school. *Educational Leadership, 51*(3), 96–97.

Million, J. (1993, October). Sexual harassers can be elementary school students. *Communicator, 17*(2), 5. Alexandria, VA: National Association of Elementary School Principals.

Modesto City Schools, CA, No. 09-93-1319 (Office for Civil Rights, U.S. Department of Education, San Francisco, Calif. Dec. 10, 1993).

Molidor, C., & Tolman, R. (1998). Gender and contextual factors in adolescent dating violence. *Violence against women, 4*(2), 180–194.

Montgomery County (MD) Public Schools, No. 03931512 (Office for Civil Rights, U.S. Department of Education, Philadelphia, Pa. Dec. 13, 1993) (letter of assurances).

Moroney, T. (1995, January 21). Coming unhinged over hand-holding ban. *Boston Globe*, pp. 1, 9.

Murray, N., & Stein, N. (1997, April 9). Dress code commentary not entirely accurate. *Education Week, 16*(28), 49.

Mutziger v. Independent School District #272 (Eden Prairie), No. ED19920006 (Minnesota Department of Human Rights Sept. 3, 1992).

Nabozny v. Podlesny, W.D. Wis., 95-C-086-S (November 19, 1996), 92 F.3d 446 (7th Cir. 1996).

Nashoba Regional School District, MA, No. 01-92-1327 (Office for Civil Rights, U.S. Department of Education, Boston, Mass. Oct. 22, 1993).

Natale, J. (1993, November). The hidden hurt. *The Executive Educator, 15*(11), 16–20.

National ACLU director enters Iowa school dispute. (1994, Summer). *The Defender, 21*(3), 3. Des Moines: Iowa American Civil Liberties Union.

New Jersey v. T.L.O, 469 U.S. 325 (1985).

Newark Unified School District, CA, No. 09-93-1113 (Office for Civil Rights, U.S. Department of Education, San Francisco, Calif. July 7, 1993).

Nolin, M. J., Davies, E., & Chandler, K. (1995, October). *Student victimization at school*. Washington, DC: U.S. Department of Education Publication (National Center for Education Statistics No. 95-204).

O'Connell, P., Sedighdeilami, F., Pepler, D. J., Craig, W., Connolly, J., Atlas, R., Smith, C., & Charach, A. (1997, April). *Prevalence of bullying and victimization among Canadian elementary and middle school children*. Poster session presented at the Society for Research on Child Development, Washington, DC.

OCR guidance on requests for confidentiality (1997, August). *Educator's Guide for Controlling Sexual Harassment, 4*(11), 7.

O'Donnell, T. R. (1994, April 27). Ames officials cluck at students' T-shirts, *Des Moines Register*, pp. 1M, 6M.

O'Keefe, N. K., Brockopp, N., & Chew, E. (1986, November–December). Teen dating violence. *Social Work, 31*(6), 465–468.

Oliver, R., Hazler, R., & Hoover, J. (1994). The perceived role of bullying in small-town midwestern schools. *Journal of Counseling and Development, 72*(4), 416–420.

Olson v. Independent School District #112, No. ED360-GSS/RP-5 (Minnesota Department of Human Rights May 21, 1991).

Olweus, D. (1993). *Bullying at school: What we know and what we can do.* Oxford: Blackwell.

Olweus, D. (1994). Annotation: Bullying at school: Basic facts and effects of a school based intervention program. *Journal of Child Psychology and Psychiatry, 35,* 1171–1190.

Oona v. McCaffrey, 143 F.3d 473 (9th Cir. 1998). & 122 F.3d 1207, 1997

Opinions in sexual harassment case. (1998). *Education Week, 17*(42), 31.

Orenstein, P. (1994). *SchoolGirls,* New York: Doubleday.

O'Toole, L. (1997, August). *It was only an innocent kiss: On the use, mis-use and non-use of context in public discussion of sexual harassment.* Paper presented at Sixth Annual Sociologists Against Sexual Harassment Conference, Toronto, CA.

O'Toole, L., & Schiffman, J. (1997). Conceptualizing gender violence. In L. O'Toole & J. Schiffman, *Gender violence: Interdisciplinary perspectives* (pp. xi–xiv). New York: New York University Press.

Palmer, J. (1994, April 20). Attire mocking Hooters T-shirts leads to suspension, *Iowa State Daily*, pp. 1–2.

Peller, G. (1993, July 25). Blackboard jungle '93: Coping with groping and worse. For girls, high school sometimes feels like Tailhook. *Washington Post*, p. C3.

People for the American Way. (1990). *Attacks on the freedom to learn, the 1989-90 Report.* Washington, DC: Author.

Pepler, D., Craig, W., Zeigler, S., & Charach, A. (1993). A school-based anti-bullying intervention: Preliminary evaluation. In D. Tattum (Ed.), *Understanding and managing bullying* (pp. 76–91). Oxford: Heinemann Educational.

Pera, G. (1996, September 6–8). The great divide: Teens and the gender gap. *USA Weekend*, pp. 10, 12–16.

Perlstein, D. (1998, Fall). Saying the unsaid: Girl killing and the curriculum. *Journal of Curriculum and Supervision, 14*(1), 88–104.

Permanent Commission (CT) on the Status of Women (1995). *In our own backyard: Sexual harassment in Connecticut's public high schools.* Hartford, CT: Author.

Pirog-Good, M. A., & Stets, J. E. (Eds.) (1989). *Violence in dating relationships: Emerging social issues.* New York: Praeger.

Pitsch, M. (1994a, November 9). OCR may review boy-on-boy sexual harassment case. *Education Week, 14*(10), 15, 20.

Pitsch, M. (1994b, November 9). OCR stepping up civil-rights enforcement. *Education Week, 14*(10), 15, 20.

Pitsch, M. (1995, June 21). A force to be reckoned with. *Education Week, 14*(39), 28–35.

Potopowitz, B. (1995). Sexual harassment a serious problem for Connecticut high school students (January 26, 1995), Connecticut Permanent Commission on the Status of Women (press release). Hartford, CT: Author.

Pupil Nondiscrimination Law (Wis. Stat. § 118.13) (1985).

Pyle v. South Hadley School Committee, 861 F. Supp. 157 (D. Mass. 1994), 55 F.3d 20 (1st Cir. 1955), *sub nom* Jeffrey J. Pyle and another v. School Committee of South Hadley and others, 423 Mass. 283 (1996).

Pyle, C. (1994). Coed naked censorship: They do it in South Hadley. Unpublished manuscript, p. 11.

Pyle, J. (1994, Autumn). Court permits school to censor "vulgar" expression. *Bill of Rights Network, 7*, 7. Boston: Massachusetts Civil Liberties Union Foundation.

Pyle, J. J., & Pyle, J. H. (1997, April 23). Opinions on dress codes from both sides of the courtroom. *Education Week, 16*(30), 49.

Quiroga, J. (1997, November 5). *News Center Five: 11 p.m. Newscast,* Boston: WCVB.

Ratcliffe, K. (1996, July). Five girls fight back. *Seventeen,* 110-113, 116.

Reis, B. (1997, Fall). *The fourth annual Safe Schools report of the Anti-Violence Documentation Project from the Safe Schools Coalition of Washington.* Seattle: Safe Schools Coalition.

Rhode Island Board of Regents policy statement on discrimination based on sexual orientation (Peter McWalters, Commissioner), May 30, 1997.

Rigby, K., Slee, P., & Conolly, C. (1991). Victims and bullies in school communities. *Journal of the Australian Society of Victimology, 1*, 25-31.

Robertson, C., Dyer, C., & Campbell, D. (1988, Summer). Campus harassment: Sexual harassment policies and procedures at institutions of higher learning. *Signs: Journal of Women in Culture and Society, 13*(4), 792-812.

Rollenhagen, E. (1994, October). Shirting the issue. *Seventeen, 53*(10), 122-123.

Roscoe, B., & Callahan, J. (1985, Fall). Adolescents' self-report of violence in families and dating relationships. *Adolescence, 29*(79), 545-553.

Roscoe, B., & Kelsey, T. (1986). Dating violence among high school students. *Psychology, 23*(1), 53-57.

Roscoe, B., Strouse, J., & Goodwin, M. (1994, Fall). Sexual harassment: Early adolescents' self-reports of experiences and acceptance. *Adolescence, 20*(115), 515-523.

Rosen, M. D. (1993, September). The big issue: Sexual harassment. *Ladies Home Journal,* 108-118.

Ross, D. M. (1996). *Childhood bullying and teasing: What school personnel, other professionals, and parents can do.* Alexandria, VA: American Counseling Association.

Rowe, M. P. (1981, May/June). Dealing with sexual harassment. *Harvard Business Review, 59*(3), 42-46.

Rowinshy v. Bryan (TX) Independent School District, 80 F.3d 1006 (5th Cir. 1996).

Rubenstein, C. (1993, June 10). Fighting sexual harassment in schools. *New York Times,* p. C8.

Ruenzel, D. (1999, April 14). Pride and prejudice. *Education Week, 18*(31), 34-39.

Russo, H. (1996). *Girls with disabilities and sexual harassment at school.* Unpublished manuscript.

Saltzman, A. (1993, December 6). It's not just teasing: Sexual harassment starts young. *U.S. News and World Report, 115*(22), 73-77.

Sauk Rapids-Rice School District #47, MN, No. 05-93-1142 (Office for Civil Rights, U.S. Department of Education, Chicago, Ill. June 23, 1993).

Schneder, B., & Jeffery, T. (producers). (1996, December). *Stand against fear.* A Moment of Truth Productions.

School district reaches settlement with former student for over $900,000. (1997, February). *Educator's Guide to Controlling Sexual Harassment, 4*(5), 1-2.

School's reaction to hazing raises free speech issues. (1996, May 17). *School Law News, 24*(10), 5-6.

Seal, K. (1994, February 14). Sexual harassment in the schools. What's the problem? *First for women, 6*(7), 92-93.

Seamons v. Snow, 864 F. Supp. 1111 (D. Utah 1994).

Seligman, K. (1996, November 17). Boys join list of the sexually harassed. *San Francisco Examiner*, pp. 1, 16.

Seppa, N. (1996, October). Bullies spend less time with adults. *APA Monitor, 24*(10), p. 41.

Sexual harassment in a New Jersey high school: A replication study (1995, Fall). *New Jersey Equity Research Bulletin, 15*, 1-4.

Sexual harassment is rampant in Texas schools, civil rights study shows (1997, December). *Educator's Guide to Controlling Sexual Harassment, 5*(3), 1, 5-6.

Shakeshaft, C. (1997, March). *Peer harassment and the culture of schooling: What administrators need to know.* Paper presented at American Educational Research Association conference, Chicago, IL.

Shakeshaft, C. (1997, October). Boys call me cow. *Educational Leadership, 5*(2), 22-25.

Shannon, S. (1993, November). Why girls don't want to go to school. *Working mother, 16*(119), 58-64.

Sherrod, L. (1993, January 20). Vance studies harassment complaints. Alleged assaults at Blair draw attention to policy. *The Silver Springs [MD] Record*, pp. 1, 16.

Sherrod, L. (1994, January 5). Blair sexual harassment investigation closed. *The Burtonsville [MD] Gazette*, pp. 1, 12.

Simbro, W. (1996, June 9). Jury sides with teen-ager, Broader issues remain in harassment verdict. *Des Moines Register*, pp. 1A, 2A.

Sjostrom, L., & Stein, N. (1996). *Bullyproof: A teacher's guide on teaching and bullying for use with fourth and fifth grade students.* Wellesley, MA: Wellesley College Center for Research on Women.

Smith, B. (1994, April). *Educating Black girls: When and why to speak or hold your tongue.* Paper presented at the annual meeting of the American Educational Research Association, New Orleans, LA.

Sneed, M., & Woodruff, K. (1994). *Sexual harassment: The complete guide for administrators.* Arlington, VA: American Association of School Administrators.

Spaid, E. L. (1993a, January 21). Schools grapple with peer harassment. *The Christian Science Monitor*, p. 3.

Spaid, E. L. (1993b, June 2). Sexual harassment found in US schools. *The Christian Science Monitor*, p. 7.

Spate of sexual assaults in bathrooms raises liability questions. (1997, December). *Educator's Guide to Controlling Sexual Harassment, 5*(3), 1-3.

Staruk, D. (1994, October 27). Andover High student arrested for disturbing school: ACLU may come to her defense, *Andover [MA] Townsman*, pp. 2, 64.

Stein, N. (Ed.). (1979, revised 1982, 1983, & 1986). *Who's hurt and who's liable: Sexual harassment in Massachusetts schools.* Malden, MA: Massachusetts Department of Education.

Stein, N. (1981). *Sexual harassment of high school students: Preliminary research results.* Boston, MA: Massachusetts Department of Education, unpublished manuscript.

Stein, N. (1991, November 27). It happens here, too: Sexual harassment in the school. *Education Week, 11*(13), 32.

Stein, N. (1992a). *Secrets in public: Sexual harassment in public (and private) schools.* (Working Paper No. 256). Wellesley, MA: Wellesley College Center for Research on Women.

Stein, N. (1992b, May/June). Sexual harassment and schools. *Rethinking Schools, 6*(4), 5-6.

Stein, N. (1992c, November 4). Sexual harassment—an update. *Education Week, 12*(9), 37.

Stein, N. (1993a). No laughing matter: Sexual harassment in K-12 schools. In E. Buchwald, P. R. Fletcher, & M. Roth, *Transforming a rape culture* (311-331). Minneapolis, MN: Milkweed Editions.

Stein, N. (1993b). It happens here, too: Sexual harassment and child sexual abuse in elementary and secondary schools. In S. K. Biklen & D. Pollard, *Gender and Education: 92nd yearbook of the National Society for the Study of Education* (pp. 191-203). Chicago: University of Chicago Press.

Stein, N. (1993c, January). Sexual harassment in the schools. *School Administrator, 1*(50), 14-21.

Stein, N. (1993d, October 18). It breaks your soul and brings you down. *New York Teacher, 35*(4), 23. New York: New York State United Teachers.

Stein, N. (1995a, Summer). Sexual harassment in K-12 schools: The public performance of gendered violence. *Harvard Educational Review, 65*(2), 145-162.

Stein, N. (1995b, June). Is it sexually charged, sexually hostile, or the Constitution? Sexual harassment in K-12 schools. *West's Education Law Reporter, 98*(2), 621-631.

Stein, N. (1996, May). Slippery justice. *Educational Leadership, 53*, 64-68.

Stein, N. (1997). *Bullying and sexual harassment in elementary schools: It's not just kids kissing kids.* (Working Paper No. 284). Wellesley, MA: Wellesley College Center for Research on Women.

Stein, N. (1999). Public/private rules. *Education Week, 18*(22), 36.

Stein, N., & Cappello, D. (1999). *Gender violence/gender justice: An interdisciplinary teaching guide for teachers of English, literature, social studies, psychology, health, peer counseling, and family and consumer sciences (grades 7-12).* Wellesley, MA: Wellesley College Center for Research on Women.

Stein, N., Marshall, N., & Tropp, L. (1993). *Secrets in public: Sexual harassment in our schools. A report on the results of a* Seventeen *magazine survey.* Wellesley, MA: Wellesley College Center for Research on Women.

Stein, N., & Sjostrom, L. (1994). *Flirting or hurting? A teacher's guide on student to student sexual harassment in grades 6–12*. Washington, DC: National Education Association Professional Library.

Stern v. City of Milford Board of Education (Super. Ct., Judicial District of Ansonia/Milford, filed Jan. 29, 1993).

Stoneking v. Bradford Area School District, 882 F.2d 720 (3rd Cir. 1989).

Stratton, S., & Backes, J. (1997, February/March). Sexual harassment in North Dakota public schools: A study of eight high schools. *High School Journal, 80*, 163–172.

Strauss, S. (1988, March). Sexual harassment in the school: Legal implications for principals. *Bulletin, 72*(506), 93–97. Reston, VA: National Association of Secondary School Principals.

Student failed to show school district's intent to discriminate in peer sexual harassment case (1997, January). *Educator's Guide to Controlling Sexual Harassment, 4*(4), 1–3.

Students blue over "mooning" (1997, April 16). *Education Week, 16*(29), 4.

Students claim school dress code violates freedom of expression (1996, October). *School Law Bulletin, 23*(10), 3–4.

Study calls schools lax on sexual harassment (1993, March 24). *Wall Street Journal*, p. 8.

Suit proceeds against individual officials for failing to stop sexual harassment (1997, October). *Educator's Guide to Controlling Sexual Harassment, 5*(1), 1, 5.

Sullivan, K. (1993, January 15). Harassment complaints grip school. Officials at Blair High face student protest, threat of 2nd lawsuit. *Washington Post*, pp. D1, 6.

Supreme Court to hear harassment case stemming from teacher-student relationship (1998, February). *Educator's Guide to Controlling Sexual Harassment, 5*(5), 1, 5–6.

Tattum, D. P. (Ed.). (1993). *Understanding and managing bullying.* Oxford: Heinemann.

Tattum, D. P., & Lane, D. A. (Eds.). (1988). *Bullying in schools.* Stoke-on-Trent: Trentham Books.

Tattum, D. P., & Tattum, E. (1997). *Bullying in the early years.* London: Gulbenkian Foundation.

Terry, D. (1996, March 29). Suit says schools failed to protect a gay student. *New York Times*, p. A14.

Texas Civil Rights Project (1997, October). *Peer sexual harassment: A Texas-size problem.* Austin, TX: Author.

Thorne, B. (1993). *Gender Play: Girls and boys in school.* New Brunswick, NJ: Rutgers University Press.

Tinker v. Des Moines School District, 393 U.S. 503, 509 (1969).

Trigg, M., & Wittenstrom, K. (1996). That's the way the world goes: Sexual harassment and New Jersey teenagers. *Initiatives, 57*(2), 55–65.

U.S. Department of Education, National Center for Education Statistics. (1998). *Violence and discipline problems in U.S. public schools: 1996–1997*, by S. Heaviside, C. Rowland, C. Williams, & E. Ferris and Westat, Inc. Washington, DC: Author.

U.S. Department of Education, Office for Civil Rights. (1997a, March 13). *Sexual harassment guidance: Harassment of students by school employees, other students, or third parties*; Notice (62 Federal Register 12034-12051).

U.S. Department of Education, Office for Civil Rights. (1997b, March). *Sexual harassment: It's not academic*. Washington, DC: Author.

Viadero, D. (1997, May 28). Bullies beware. *Education Week, 16*(35), 19-21.

Wagner, V., & Coats, R. (1992, December 6). Schools hope programs will teach students respect. *Modesto Bee*, p. F3.

Walsh, M. (1994, October 19). Harassment suit rejected. *Education Week, 14*(7), 10.

Walsh, M. (1996a, May 8). Districts cannot be held liable for student harassment, court rules. *Education Week, 15*(33), 7.

Walsh, M. (1996b, September 25). In harassment suits, a new era emerges. *Education Week, 16*(4), 1, 14.

Walsh, M. (1997a, Jan. 15). Law update. *Education Week, 16*(16), 9.

Walsh, M. (1997b, September 3). Federal courts split over schools' responsibility for peer sexual harassment. *Education Week, 17*(1), 8.

Walsh, M. (1998a, July 8). District agrees to protect gay students. *Education Week, 17*(42), 30.

Walsh, M. (1998b, July 8). Riley restates rules against harassment. *Education Week, 17*(42), 1, 30-31.

Walsh, M. (1999, June 2). Harassment ruling poses challenges. *Education Week, 18* (38), 1, 22.

Ward, J. V. (1996). Raising resisters: The role of truth telling in the psychological development of African American girls. In B. Ross Leadbeater & N. Way, *Urban girls: Resisting stereotypes, creating identities* (pp. 85-99). New York: New York University Press.

Webb, L., Hunnicutt, D., Hartwell, K., & Metha, A. (1997, January). What schools can do to combat student-to-student sexual harassment. *NAASP Bulletin, 18*(585), 72-79.

Weiss, S. (1994, April). Flirting or hurting? *NEA Today, 12*(8), 4-5.

Whitney, I., & Smith, P. K. (1993). A survey of the nature and extent of bullying in junior/middle and secondary schools. *Educational Research, 31*(1), 3-25.

Winship, B. (1994, February 3). Teacher is wrong to dismiss boy's actions as flirting. *Boston Globe*, p. 50.

Winship, B. (1995, June 23). Picked-on students need teachers' support. *Boston Globe*, p. 54.

Wright v. Mason City (IA) School District, 940 F. Supp. 1412 (N.D. Iowa 1996).

Yaffe, E. (1995, November). Expensive, illegal, and wrong: Sexual harassment in our schools. *Phi Delta Kappan, 77*(3), K1-15.

Index

About the Author

Nan Stein is a senior research scientist at the Center for Research on Women at Wellesley College, where she directs several research projects on bullying, sexual harassment, and gender violence in K–12 schools. Since 1994, she has coauthored three teacher's guides: *Gender Violence/Gender Justice: An Interdisciplinary Teaching Guide for Teachers of English, Literature, Social Studies, Psychology, Health, Peer Counseling, and Family and Consumer Sciences (Grades 7–12)*; *Flirting or Hurting? A Teacher's Guide on Student-to-Student Sexual Harassment in Schools (for Grades 6–12)*; and *Bullyproof: A Teacher's Guide on Teasing and Bullying for Use with Fourth and Fifth Grade Students*. She has also written several book chapters and articles for academic journals as well as for the popular and education press. She has served as an expert witness in several sexual harassment lawsuits.

Dr. Stein was a middle school social studies teacher and a drug and alcohol counselor. She holds a BA in history from the University of Wisconsin, an MAT from Antioch College Graduate School of Education, and a doctorate in education from Harvard University Graduate School of Education.